SAVED BY A SONG

SAVED
BY A
SONG

The Art
and Healing Power
of Songwriting

MARY GAUTHIER

ST. MARTIN'S
ESSENTIALS
NEW YORK

First published in the United States by St. Martin's Essentials, an imprint of St. Martin's Publishing Group

www.stmartins.com

The Library of Congress Cataloging-in-Publication Data is available upon request.

ISBN 978-1-250-20211-6 (hardcover)
ISBN 978-1-250-20212-3 (ebook)

First Edition: 2021

10 9 8 7 6 5 4 3 2 1

I dedicate this book to Jaimee, my love, who has patiently allowed me to carve out the time to write these words. I am grateful to have a partner who believes in me, encourages me, and supports my efforts with patience and kindness, and who mercifully forgives me when I screw up. I screw up a lot. May we continue to work out the meaning of love, together.

Contents

If you bring forth what is within you, what you bring forth will save you. If you do not bring forth what is within you, what you do not bring forth will destroy you.

—Gospel of Thomas

SAVED BY A SONG

INVITATION

Where do songs come from? I'm not sure, really. I learned how to write songs by writing them. I quit high school and college, I didn't go to music school, and I don't like following directions. It's my nature to challenge authority, do things my own way. I call my stubbornness "entrepreneurial." But I'm willing to listen when I'm given a choice. Deb, my beloved therapist of many years, found a workaround for me: When offering me a suggestion, she says, "Mary, I would like to invite you to consider . . ." It works.

So this book is a collection of stories, observations, and ideas I'm inviting you to consider. It's also a behind-the-curtain glimpse into my life and my songwriting process. It's not a rule book. Even if I was interested in rules, I don't know of a single songwriting rule that can be universally applied. There are no absolutes in songwriting, and no one holds a monopoly on how it should be done.

My friend and fellow songwriter Lori McKenna says writing a song can be like chasing a wounded bird down a road. It never goes in the direction you expect. It leads you more than you realize, but then it may suddenly take off. The song becomes bigger than you imagined and rewards you with its strength. The challenge is learning how to catch a wounded bird without damaging it.

Over the years, I've had hundreds of hair-raising moments when the bird I was chasing took flight. Understanding what happens in those moments, how songwriting actually works, well, that occurs in retrospect, if at all. I start at the beginning every single time. Even after thirty years, the art of song remains mysterious to me.

Writing songs helps me sort out confusion, untangle powerful emotions, and ward off desperation. It helps me navigate the powerful emotional weather systems of life. When the storms come, as they always do, they provide genuine songwriting motivation. After the wind dies down and the water recedes, I'm driven to try and make sense of what happened, try to make meaning out of what at first glance appears to be chaos. I write songs because I am called to. Songwriting gives me a reason to get up in the morning. It is a godsend.

I try to return that gift by teaching. I've worked with a couple of teachers myself (my friend Ralph Murphy comes to mind), all of them committed to passing knowledge from one generation to the next. That said, I'm not sure songwriting can be "taught" in a classic sense. As my friend and fellow teacher Verlon Thompson says, "I'm not a songwriting teacher. I'm a song encourager." Yeah, me too. My hope is to encourage courage.

I started encouraging other songwriters when I was asked to at a folk festival in Colorado, then again at another music festival in Canada. Word got around I was a "teacher" and I became one. I work with songwriters who make a living with their songs, others who hope to, and many who simply want to be better writers. I've worked with thousands of people, and I've yet to meet a single one called to songwriting by mistake. The calling knows what it is doing when it taps someone on the shoulder and whispers, "Write." There's divine wisdom in the beckoning. A song waiting to be born has something to teach the songwriter, something we didn't know before we wrote it.

Novelist and essayist James Baldwin once remarked that the act of writing is "finding out what you don't want to know, what you don't want to find out." This is true for me. I write in the dark of unknowing, searching for the light of understanding. If I find the switch and the light comes on, my song could serve to illuminate something for myself and, perhaps, for others. Like meditation and prayer, songwriting can be a spiritual practice. Either way, illumination is a positive force, a win.

Beyond reason and conscious thought, past my own story, behind firewalls of self-protection and fear, sits a mysterious power that turns a good song into a great one. I've sat for hours trying to figure out a song, hopelessly stuck. My best writing happens in a kind of trance, an exercise in faith. I only know I've gotten "there" in retrospect, when the words and melody do more than I imagined possible when I put them together.

I am not in charge of the flow. All I can do is show up, direct focused effort, and hope the mystery will assist. The process is often about emptying my mind until I can access the state of consciousness where I'm not writing but feeling and listening. Sometimes that state of consciousness eludes me completely, leaving me frustrated.

So, I'll walk away.

Let it rest.

Try again tomorrow.

This is what it's like to be a songwriter.

Honestly, it can be an ordeal.

As the great country songwriter Harlan Howard used to say, "He writes the songs. I hold the pen."

People ask me if I believe songs can change the world. My answer is yes, absolutely. Here's how: A song can change a heart by creating empathy. A changed heart has the power to change a mind. And when a mind changes, a person changes. When people change, the world changes. One song, one heart, one mind, one person at a time. Songs can bring us a deeper understanding of each other and ourselves and open the heart to love.

There are many wonderful books on song craft and hit writing, but this book takes its aim at what makes a song matter. Analysis of technique and structure aside, I believe songs that heal come from a higher place. They help us with the struggle of being human by letting us know we are not alone. This is the greatest gift a song can give a songwriter and a songwriter can give the world.

Bruce Springsteen said, "Music is a repair shop. I'm basically a repair man." I love that. Songs have the power to repair hearts and heal souls.

Saved by a song.

One

I DRINK:
REDUCTION

I Drink

He'd get home at 5:30, fix his drink
And sit down in his chair
Pick a fight with mama,
Complain about us kids getting in his hair
At night he'd sit alone and smoke
I'd see his frown behind his lighter's flame
Now that same frown's in my mirror
I got my daddy's blood inside my veins

Fish swim birds fly
Daddies yell mamas cry
Old men sit and think
I drink

Chicken TV dinner
Six minutes on defrost three on high
A beer to wash it down with
Then another, a little whiskey on the side
It's not so bad alone here
It don't bother me that every night's the same
I don't need another lover
Hanging round, trying to make me change

Fish swim birds fly
Daddies yell mamas cry

Old men sit and think
I drink

I know what I am
But I don't give a damn

Fish swim birds fly
Daddies yell mamas cry
Old men sit and think
I drink

—Mary Gauthier and Crit Harmon

There was a loud burst of a police siren, flashing blue lights in my rearview.

It was dark, late.

Bars had closed.

The streets were quiet.

I was drunk.

I pulled over, rolled down the window. Waited.

A cop beamed his flashlight directly into my eyes.

"You're driving erratically. I've been following you for ten minutes. How many drinks have you had?"

"Uh . . . well, I had a couple, maybe two?"

"Oh yeah? License and registration."

I handed him my license, fumbled around the glove box, couldn't find the registration. The cop lost patience.

"Step out of the car."

"Put your left pointer finger to your nose."

Left . . . pointer finger . . . to my nose, damn it . . . not easy.

"Right pointer finger, to your nose."

Effort, it took so much effort, to put my pointer finger to my nose.

"Stand on one leg. Count to five."

I made it to two.

"Recite the alphabet backwards."

I only had Z and Y.

The cop smirked, shook his head, rested his hand on his holster, and stared. Was he making fun of me?

"Look, man, either arrest me or let me go."

The snapping sound of latex gloves.

"Put your hands behind your back."

He cuffed me tightly, then opened the back door of the cruiser. I was too drunk to get into the back of the police car with my hands cuffed behind my back. He steadied me, then tossed me into the car. Slammed the door.

I blacked out.

Someone shook me awake. "We're at the station. Get up."

I remember bright fluorescent lights. Being frisked. My pockets were emptied. A strong hand grabbed my fingers and smashed them one at a time into black fingerprint ink, then onto paper cards.

I was led to a holding cell.

The door slammed shut, then locked.

The lights went out.

I was alone in the pitch-black. I felt my way with my hands, found a bench along the wall. I tried to lie down. Too small. I fell off. Stayed on the floor. Blacked out.

I woke up. Had it been minutes? Hours?

I moved my hands along the floor, felt a hole in the cement next to my face. Sticky. The stench of old urine. The hole was a toilet.

I left my body.

I looked down at myself from the ceiling, on the floor in a fetal position. A millisecond of clarity as denial lifted.

I saw myself. I had a problem, a serious problem. I mut-
tered, maybe thought, "Help me. Please, please, help me."
I meant it.

I blacked out again.

The light came back on, the door opened. A female
officer entered. She put on rubber gloves. "Cavity search.
Pull down your pants. Bend over." She puts her finger in
me, front, then back. I felt nothing.

"Let's go. You can make a phone call."

I called my business partner and investor, Tom. Tonight
was the opening night of our second restaurant, the Dixie
Kitchen, a ninety-six-seat Louisiana-style restaurant on
Mass. Ave in Boston. Tom called his friend, a high-powered
lawyer whose name I recognized from TV, who immediately called me back and told me to refuse the breath test,
keep my mouth shut, and find an employee who would
testify under oath that I was not drinking. He directed me
to go back into my cell till they let me out in the morning. He said I could pay him 15K up front and another 15K
when he got me out of this mess. I said thank you, hung
up. Asked for another call. The cop nodded ok.

I called my ex-lover. An hour or so later, she showed up
with her new girlfriend. They put up bail. I signed papers.
The cops retrieved my belongings.

The sun was coming up as we left the station. No one
spoke. I sat alone in the back seat. They drove me to the
tow lot, dropped me off at the gate. I paid the attendant.
Walked across the gravel lot, got in my car, drove home.

I lay down, slept two hours.

Woke up still drunk, filthy. My arraignment was in an hour.

I had a massive, full-body hangover. I moaned. I wanted to die. I made myself get up, take a shower, get dressed, drive to the courthouse. I took a court-appointed attorney.

The attorney leaned in to speak. I backed away. Couldn't let him near me. I felt despicable, repulsive. My pores reeked of booze. His voice rose up through the bustling din of the crowded courthouse lobby, then disappeared like smoke into the skylight. I could not focus on his words. I could not even look at him. I was in throbbing, visceral pain.

"Do whatever you think is right. I don't care. Just get me out of here." No more lying. No more running. I didn't know I'd had a spiritual experience in the jail cell. I wasn't aware that Grace had entered my life. But from the moment I truly saw myself laying on the floor of that holding cell, my life changed. Brutalized by the truth, I hung my head and surrendered. It was the bottom, the end, but also, like all endings, it was a new beginning.

My drunk driving case was continued without a finding. In the eyes of the court I was neither innocent nor guilty. I was assigned a probation officer and ordered to check in once a month for a year. I was court ordered to a weekly twelve-step program. The next night, Michael, a waiter at my new restaurant who'd help me design and set up the waiters' stations, took me to a twelve-step recovery meeting next door at Berklee College of Music.

Bloated and exhausted, with dark circles under my bloodshot eyes, overweight from years of heavy drinking, I looked like a middle-aged alcoholic short-order cook with an anger problem. People stayed clear.

The chairperson read "How It Works." I'd not heard it since I was a teenager. I thought about my failed attempts to get sober when I was young, my multiple treatment center stays before I was eighteen, halfway houses, my overdose. Memories came flooding in, and I felt the push of tears. Emotion felt strange, foreign. I hadn't cried in years.

It was July 13, 1990. I was twenty-eight years old.

I have not had a drink or drug since.

My mind, body, and spirit were raging. I was terrified, self-conscious, self-critical, self-centered. I felt removed, like there was a two-inch plate of bulletproof glass between me and other people. Booze and dope had helped me act human and temporarily break through the glass. Sober, I had no idea what do. An addict who has stopped using is not an addict without a problem. My internal organs felt exposed, and I had no protection. Sober, I was going to have to contend with the godforsaken hole, the distance, aching to be filled.

A year before I got arrested for drunk driving, I was headed home from work on I-95 in my dirty chef's coat with the radio on. I was almost home when WUMB played a song that got my attention. I'd not heard the singer before, but her deep voice grabbed me. She sang,

I come to you with strange fire
I make an offering of love

I pulled into my driveway, shut the car off, and turned the radio up. Another female voice sang harmonies, and the sound of these combined voices kicked open a trap door somewhere inside me, exposing a personal Pompeii, an ancient, buried city that was once vibrant and alive. The song made me hurt, but I could not understand why. I also could not stop listening. What the hell was this awful feeling? Longing? For what? I sat with my eyes closed. The DJ said the duo called themselves the Indigo Girls, the song—"Strange Fire."

I turned the radio off, clenched the steering wheel with both hands, put my head on it. Then, I banged my hands on it. Hard, then harder.

For as long as I could remember, there had been an emptiness eating away at me. I tried to fill it with booze and dope and sex and food and money. I'd worked my way into something good in Boston, I went to chef school, found investors, opened restaurants. I was young, successful, and had what I thought I wanted. But I was miserable.

Whatever the song on the radio was trying to tell me made no sense. It just reminded me of how lost I was. I got out of my truck, slammed the door, went inside, made a strong drink, and got high.

After I got sober the feelings that song brought up continued to haunt me. I thought about it, a lot. I saw a poster advertising the Indigo Girls playing at the Paradise Rock Club. I bought a ticket.

I got there early, had to wait in line to get in. The show was sold out, and the club was humming with excitement. I went straight to the bar to get a mineral water, then headed for the back of the room, to stand against the wall. When the Indigo Girls took the stage, the predominantly female audience exploded in raw emotion and rushed toward the stage, screaming, crying. I'd never seen anything like it. Women screaming for women. The fans were filled with an erotic panic, a pulling-their-hair-out kind of excitement. It reminded me of the black-and-white footage of girls screaming for the Beatles in '64. I did not know it yet, but "Closer to Fine" was climbing the charts, soon to be a smash hit. The Indigo Girls were on their way to becoming icons. Lesbian icons.

For most of my life, the thought of such a thing would have been laughable. In my teens, when I began to wonder if I was gay, I went to the library looking for lesbian authors. My research brought me to one book, Radclyffe Hall's *Well of Loneliness,* published in England in 1928. I read it, then landed on its successor, the bimonthly mailed-in-a-plain-brown-paper-wrapper lesbian newsletter *LC,* the *Lesbian Connection.* As a nod to Hall's book, the polite *LC* personal ads were called "The Wishing Well." *LC* introduced me to "womyn's" music—music by women, for women, and about women. I volunteered at a womyn's music festival outside of Atlanta with my first girlfriend when I was eighteen. I didn't know what I was expecting, but the lesbian-feminist-separatist vibe was intense. It was bossy, which I did not and do not like. I did discover the brilliant Canadian folk singer Ferron there, but I was young and full of angst, and most of the music at the womyn's festival did not speak to me. At the time, I preferred music with thrust, rebellion, raw emotion. Artists like Lou Reed, Patti Smith,

Bowie, Iggy Pop, Green on Red, the Violent Femmes. Waylon and Willie and The Outlaws were my constants.

That night at the Paradise Rock Club, as I watched women jump up and down and scream their lungs out for the two obviously queer women on stage with unapologetic out-ness and joy, I knew the world was changing.

But something was wrong inside me. I had the same feeling I'd had in my truck, but worse. I went to the women's bathroom, closed myself inside a stall. I was covered in cold sweat and dizzy. For a moment, I thought I would be sick. It wasn't the queerness in the room that freaked me out. I'd been out for years. It was something else. I had no idea what, but I had to get the hell out of there.

I had not yet written my first song, but the rise of the Indigo Girls in popular music was prying something open in me. A repressed, buried part of myself was starting to stir. It was the pain of an unlived life, of course, but I did not know that, yet.

A few months later, Christy, a Berklee music school student who waited tables at Dixie Kitchen, invited me to come hear her play one of her songs at an open mic at Club Passim, the old folk club in Harvard Square. I'd been to Passim before, but I'd never heard of an open mic. I was intrigued. Christy explained an "open mic" was open to any songwriter who paid the fee to get in. They set the stage up "in the round," like The Bluebird Cafe in Nashville, where songwriters sat in a circle of chairs and swapped songs. Thirty or forty songwriters showed up at Passim every Tuesday, three songwriters took the stage, each played an original song. No auditions, everyone was welcome. Pay five bucks and play. Names drawn from a hat. Christy said open mics were a way to move original songs to their first audience, a good starting place. We took the T to Cambridge, paid at the door, and Christy put her name on the list.

The café was full of determined occupants of an underground scene, all waiting to take the stage. A joyful hum filled the air; they all knew each other. There were guitars, lyric sheets, and instrument cases everywhere. We grabbed a table in the back and ordered some coffee.

When they called Christy's name, she walked on stage, sat behind the piano, and transformed from the waitress I thought I knew into a confident, poised performer. It was incredible. I was proud of her and blown away by her courage and her beautiful song. I had no idea she had it in her.

A deep knowing overtook me. THIS IS IT! I want to do this. In fact, I'd ALWAYS wanted to do this! The urge to write songs had been inside me since I was twelve years old, when my aunt Jenny gave me her old Guild guitar. I loved that guitar, learned chords from a Mel Bay basic guitar workbook. Then I learned songs off the radio, even tried to write one of my own a couple times. I had always loved songs. I even took piano lessons when I was a kid. My teacher was a nun at St. Joseph's Academy for girls in Baton Rouge. Once a week, I'd climb the five flights of stairs to her office and knock on her closed door, winded. A soft voice would say, "Mary Veronica, please come in."

Sr. Augusta was small in stature, gentle, kind, and elderly, a sister of St. Joseph. Her tiny teaching studio felt like being trapped inside an old lady's purse—Kleenex, face powder, pennies, and lint.

When I entered, Sister would be sitting primly on the piano bench. She wore a light brown habit, with large wooden rosary beads around her neck. Her crucifix would sway when she patted the small empty spot on the piano bench beside her, motioning for me to sit. I'd take my seat and instinctively adjust my Catholic schoolgirl skirt downward. I was athletic, high-strung, and, even at age ten, bigger than Sr. Augusta. Sitting next to her made me nervous.

She'd pull sheet music from her file drawer and put it on the music stand, lift her scary blue-veined hands with translucent corpselike skin and rest them on the keys. Eyes closed, she'd sit silently for a moment then open her eyes and start the lesson, sight-reading the prior week's song. As the last note from the old upright faded, she'd sit back and grab her pointer.

My turn.

The notes and music I should have studied sat in front of me, foreign. The flash cards designed to help beginning sight-readers sat unopened on the dresser in my bedroom. I did not do my homework.

But when Sr. Augusta placed the tip of her pointer on the first note of the sheet music, I played. Eyes on the notes, pretending to read, I faked it. The music on the page remained a dizzying blur as I re-created from memory what she had demonstrated. I'd think of the flash cards, wishing I'd studied. But my ear worked music out for me back then. Still does.

My relationship with Sr. Augusta was short lived. I

didn't have the patience or desire to read music. Plus, the songs I loved on the radio seemed to have no relation to piano lessons with a sweet old nun. Sr. Augusta did not engage my imagination, and I quit piano lessons.

I'd revisit the urge to write songs every now and then, pull out my guitar and try to come up with something, but I eventually moved on. I went to chef school, went into the restaurant business, worked all the time, and drank.

Sitting in that little wooden café chair in Passim that night, I knew I wanted to write a song and play it on the stage of Club Passim.

When I got home, I pulled out my old Ovation round-back guitar. I hadn't touched it in years. I had a pack of strings in the case, so I restrung it. I began fumbling with simple chord changes. Over the next few weeks, I built calluses on my fingers and began working on a song. I'd write early in the morning before work and rush home after work to write in the evening.

I went to Passim every Tuesday. Songwriters showed up, signed up, and, when their name was called, played. From my seat in the back of the room, it seemed easy.

Weeks went by and I kept working on my song, my hands on my guitar for hours, until they ached. I wrote and rewrote. I played in front of a mirror, strummed like hell, and sang at the top of my voice. I recorded my efforts on a handheld recorder and listened back. Not great. Still needed work. Months went by.

I woke up one Tuesday morning and knew it was the day. I was ready. I packed my guitar, hopped in my truck, drove to Cambridge, paid the cover charge, got on the list, and took my seat. The faces were familiar now, people I'd seen and heard every week. I felt like I knew them, but they didn't know me, yet.

But it suddenly occurred to me that I was older than most all of them. This felt like a setback.

It also hit me that I was probably the only one there from the Deep South, with a southern accent. My song sounded country, and no one else sounded like that. Another setback.

Also, I was overweight from drinking and my years in the kitchen. I was heavy. Truth be told, I was probably obese.

And OMG, I looked gay. I was the gayest-looking person in the room.

They were going to hate me.

Clearly, I was making a horrible mistake being the only fat, old, southern queer to play this New England folk open mic. I considered bolting, but the host was calling out the names for the next round: ". . . and Mary Gauthier."

I was not prepared for what happened next.

My heart began to pound wildly. I stood up to get my guitar and my legs shook, they barely worked. The closer I got to the stage, the worse it got. My heart banged like timpani drums of doom in my ears.

I made it onto the stage, grabbed a chair and sat down. My hands clenched my guitar for dear life. My entire body was vibrating. I closed my eyes, took a deep breath. I forced myself to reopen my eyes, look up and out. People looked bored. No one noticed my terror. No one cared.

Holy shit, I was first.

I took a deep breath, fought back the impulse to run, forced my shaking hand onto the guitar to form a chord, then forced my other hand to strum. I started to sing, leaned in too much, and bumped my teeth on the microphone. I pulled back hard and banged my guitar against the instrument mic.

It exploded.

People in the front tables grabbed their ears.

My song, the one I'd worked on for months and practiced hundreds of times in front of a mirror, vanished. I could not remember a single word. I froze. My face went red.

Years went by.

I apologized, mumbled, "Sorry, so sorry." The room offered me a weak splattering of encouragement.

I shook my head no. I pass.

The songwriter next to me shrugged, then played his song. Mortified, I had to stay seated on that stage until the other two songwriters finished playing. When the round ended, I packed up quickly and left.

I hated myself. I wanted to disappear, dematerialize. Die? I wanted to go back to the restaurant and stay there forever. I was not a happy restaurateur anymore, but at least I knew what I was doing in a kitchen.

I had a hard time sleeping that night. I kept waking up, remembering, sinking in shame. The terror I'd felt in those excruciating minutes was beyond any fear I'd ever experienced. Stage fright felt more life-threatening than the time I'd had a loaded .357 pointed directly in my face by a lunatic in a pickup truck in a Baton Rouge biker bar parking lot.

I heard two distinct voices in my head. The loud, brutal

critic who screamed that the song I'd worked so hard on was horrible, it sucked. On top of which, I sucked. "The hell with it," that voice said, "Better you should kill yourself than ever stand on another stage again."

But there was another voice, one that whispered, "You might do better next time." It suggested that the bully in my brain might be a wee bit of an overreaction. It said, "Lighten up, you're just getting started. Practice your ass off, bring it back to Passim next Tuesday, and just get through a whole song. That's your new goal."

The bully raged for days. Getting back to the tiny encouraging whisper took time and faith. I didn't have much faith, but somehow, I forced myself back to the open mic. On my second try, I made it through a whole song. I was terrified and terrible. It was a wobbly, awful performance, but at least I remembered the words.

After a few days, when I finally quit beating the hell out of myself, I set a new goal. Show up again next week, see if I could just be a little less awful. Week after week I'd go through the cycle. I'd talk myself into signing up and playing, get on stage, and when the stage lights hit my face, I'd panic. Some nights I'd walk off stage and directly out of the building, consumed by self-loathing. Slowly, very slowly, I began to improve.

I began to try to talk about my desire to be a songwriter in my recovery meetings. I'd get flustered and stop talking midsentence.

Pass.

Speaking to a group about wanting to write songs left me exposed. I worried I was delusional, harboring an unrealistic, age-inappropriate dream. I was beginning to get real with myself and others for the first time—but sharing my heart's desires with a group filled me with an intense feeling of unworthiness.

Deep down, I was convinced my attempts at songwriting would end catastrophically, in humiliation. Fear said, "Just keep your mouth shut. Hope is dangerous. Better to keep this a secret than to fail."

Also, saying I wanted to be a songwriter was not the whole truth. My songs needed to be sung, and I'd have to be the one to sing them. As hard as it was to say I wanted to be a songwriter, it was even more difficult to claim the desire to sing. Hyper aware of the limitations of my singing voice, it took me months to say I wanted to write *and* perform my own songs.

The process was similar to coming out as a gay woman, something I'd done as a teenager. My soul was trying to integrate different parts of myself into a single self. I was grappling with integrity.

People in the meetings nodded and told me recovery was a process of gradually waking up from a deep, coma-like sleep. They said straight people get sober and find out they are gay, gay people find out they are straight, lawyers find out they are called to be actors, and, yes, restaurateurs can find out they are called to be troubadours. They said early sobriety is a time of deep discovery, a time of being amazed, of seeing the world with new eyes. They told me addiction had blocked me from the sunlight of the spirit. They said, "Keep coming."

I attended several meetings a week. Every week.

I also made myself go to Passim every Tuesday. By simply dragging my body to the place where other songwriters gathered, I created new possibilities. I made new friends. We'd congratulate each other when we did well, encourage each other when we stumbled.

It felt good, the best I had felt maybe . . . ever. Sunlight of the spirit? I wasn't basking in it. But my soul was starting to re-enter my body. I didn't know it yet, but the gaping hole in me was getting smaller.

I began writing a song I called "I Drink." I'd written several songs by that time, but this one was challenging me on a whole other level. It was slow, slow going. The plodding, time-consuming process reminded me of the process of making a classic reduction sauce, a demi-glace. Demi-glace is one of the finest sauces in French cooking and the backbone of some of the world's other greatest sauces. Making it is arduous, but when done right it's worth the effort. It's one of the basic lessons taught at culinary schools; it teaches students patience and the use of quality ingredients.

A demi-glace is made by oven roasting several pounds of veal and beef bones with onions and carrots and celery and garlic, then deglazing the brown bits in the pan with wine, then pouring it all into a stock pot. Add chopped celery, carrots, and onions; fill it with water and more wine, tomato paste, and herbs; then slowly boil it down until it becomes a thick, deep glaze. Roasted bones and vegetables boiled in twenty-odd gallons of water and a couple bottles of wine, over time, will become a few cups of amazingly rich sauce. There is no shortcut for classic demi-glace.

Reduction in songwriting means getting rid of every syllable that does not absolutely have to be there and getting to the essence of the story. Boil, simmer, reduce; boil, simmer, reduce. Reduction reveals truth. It creates compression, saying as little as possible: fewer words makes every word carry more weight.

I brought in a co-writer to help me, my friend Crit Harmon, who I'd met in a Ralph Murphy songwriting workshop two years prior. Crit had produced a record I loved, Martin Sexton's *Black Sheep*, and I asked him to help me with my first record, which he produced as more or less a demo of the songs I had written so far.

He came on board to co-write this new song with me, and we inspected each line, asking, does this feel honest? Do we really believe this? Who is speaking? Is it me, Mary Gauthier? If not, who is it? Who is the speaker addressing? Would the speaker really say that? What's going on? Here's a look at one of our early drafts:

My daddy had a good job
He wore a suit and never missed a day
Mama said don't bother him
Just go outside and play
At night he'd sit alone and smoke
I'd see his face behind the lighter's flame
I don't know what he was thinking
I've got my daddy's blood inside my veins

Fish swim, birds fly
Lovers leave by and by

Clocks tick, ice cubes clink
I drink

When love breaks down it's a terrible mess
When open arms fold in bitterness
The more I love the more I'm on the brink
Bartender please pour me a drink

Fish swim, birds fly
Lovers leave by and by
Clocks tick, ice cubes clink
I drink

I began to realize the narrator was me, but not me. It was an imagined me, a Mary who had not gotten sober and was stuck in a rundown apartment in Central Square in Cambridge, miserable and blaming her misfortunes on others. In my mind, this character was also modeled on the hard-drinking New England country singer John Lincoln Wright, whom I used to love to watch perform at the Cantab Lounge in Cambridge's Central Square. When Crit and I figured that out, it helped us to begin to boil down and reduce the verses. The first verse became purely autobiographical, a scene from my childhood:

> ~~My daddy had a good job~~ He'd get home at 5:30,
> ~~He wore a suit never missed a day~~ Fix his drink sit down in
>   his chair
> ~~Mama said don't bother him~~ Pick a fight with mama

~~Just go outside and play~~ Complain about us kids getting in
  his hair
At night he'd sit alone and smoke
I'd see his face behind the lighter's flame
~~I don't know what he was thinking~~ That same frown's in my
  mirror
I've got my daddy's blood inside my veins

The second verse was fictional, in the voice of still-drunk Mary + John Lincoln Wright:

Chicken TV dinner
six minutes on defrost three on high
Beer to wash it down with
~~Light a smoke and turn down the lights~~
Another, then some whiskey on the side
It ain't so bad alone here, don't bother that every night's the same
I don't need another lover ~~telling me~~ trying to make me ~~it's~~
  ~~time for me to~~ change

We knew we needed a bridge after the second verse before the last chorus, but we hit a wall writing it. It was the hardest two lines of the song to imagine. We tried dozens of ideas, but none felt right. There was something truer underneath, but we could not break through to it. We had a four-line bridge:

They sent me to those meetings
For my first offense

Second time it helped
But it didn't make much sense

This sentiment was vague, and four lines felt too long. Pete Seeger used to say, "Anyone can make a song complicated. It takes a real genius to keep it simple." Simple, yeah. I reduced the bridge to three lines and tried:

I don't care what they say
I ain't that bad
I see worse, every day

It was better shorter, for sure. But these words weren't right. Months went by, we kept at it. It felt like there was a deeper revelation than what we'd written. I refused to settle for less because in my gut I knew there was a bigger truth buried underneath the almost-truth that we had written.

We knew this character was in trouble with alcohol and in denial. Alcoholic denial is different than lying; this character genuinely had no idea how bad it had gotten. I wanted the character to say something that would demonstrate alcoholic denial in two short lines. Not easy.

One morning, walking, it hit me. When an addict says with emotion, "I don't give a damn!" they probably do. Pretending not to care is a deflection, it's something we do when caring is too costly. I wrote:

I know what I am, but I don't give a damn

Finally!

"I Drink" is written from the viewpoint of an alcoholic who is not interested in getting sober. This song is no "Margaritaville," there's no "nibbling on sponge cake." The party is long over. What's left is loneliness and an inevitable descent.

The stripped-down simplicity of language, the singer's matter-of-fact dry delivery, truth being told faster than the listener can keep up with, add up to a song that sometimes makes an audience laugh. But when that bridge hits, the listener understands the narrator is not well, and it's not funny anymore. It's not funny witnessing someone whose been blindsided by alcoholism.

It took nearly two years to boil down, reduce, and find the essence of this song, but our patience paid off. Complex simplicity. Now we had a chorus people could sing, and it meant more every time through. This song would become a career song for me, a door opener that would one day be covered by many other artists. Years later, Bob Dylan played it on the first installment of his *Theme Time Radio Hour* show, read the lyrics, and talked about me, introducing me to legions of his listeners all over the world.

Two

GODDAMN HIV: WRITER'S VOICE

Goddamn HIV

My name is Michael Joe Alexandry
I've been a queer since the day I was born
My family they don't say much to me,
My heart knows their silence as scorn
My friends have been dying my best friends are dead
I walk around these days with their picture in my head
Spend my time thinking 'bout things they said
I don't know what's happening to me, goddamn HIV

I don't know what all this means
I don't think it means what it seems

We used to party all night 'til the dawn
I can still see the boys with their tight leather on
In the downtown bar where it always was night
I'd hang with my friends and feel alright
I was thirty years old when the sickness first came
It rolled through my world like a wind driven flame
Leaving ashes, memories, funerals and pain
I don't know what's happening to me, goddamn HIV
I don't know what all this means
I don't think it means what it seems

When I was a boy, I'd get scared at night
My momma would come and turn on the light

But there's nobody here with me tonight
And I'm scared to close my eyes and get some sleep
Sometimes at dusk I walk the train track
I walk and I walk like I ain't coming back
I look at the sky so endless and black
Man I swear it's swallowing me, goddamn HIV

—Mary Gauthier

About a year into playing the weekly open mic at Club Passim, my friend Steve and I went to the Old Vienna Coffeehouse open mic in Westborough, Massachusetts. Steve said the Old Vienna's open mic was bigger and more high-profile than Club Passim. It was *the* place to rub shoulders with the New England songwriting community.

When we arrived, the room was packed. Amateurs signed up alongside up-and-comers, several who had record deals and songs on college radio. To me, these artists were superstars. I'd never met anyone who had a song on the radio. I was in awe.

More than eighty songwriters signed up to play. At five minutes or so per song (plus setup time), it was going to be a long night. We paid, then drew numbers, hoping for a low one. Some songwriters who drew a high number turned around and left, bummed at their bad luck. This open mic was not about listening—it was about being heard. Steve and I both drew high numbers, landing us resoundingly in the late-late pile, but we decided to stay.

Robert Haig, the MC, kicked it off with a short welcome, then introduced the first performer. One by one, they took the stage, each trying to impress the audience of other songwriters. Most were young, earnest, and far more polished than me.

By midnight, I grew restless and uncomfortable in my straight-backed wooden chair. I was considering telling Steve I wanted to call it a night when Robert introduced the next performer.

The man took the stage in dirty overalls that clung tightly to his massive belly. He wore muddy work boots and a tattered straw hat. Round-faced with puffy, crimson cheeks, his large shoulders and huge head made the straw hat look tiny. His massive belly had the same effect on his guitar. He looked like a farmer, fresh from the field. People in the back of the room held back a groan.

Robert helped him plug his guitar in. The guy immediately began strumming, hitting the strings without finesse, eyes to the floor, hands visibly shaking, offering no introduction. He looked terrified. His face grew redder as he started to sing. He began to sweat. The poor soul never looked up.

In the café, legs were crossing and recrossing, papers were shuffling. It was late. No one wanted to sit through this.

The farmer sang his way through a verse, then hit his first chorus:

> Got holes I can't fill, bills I can't pay,
> I'm gonna walk in the water 'til my hat floats away

I looked at Steve. Steve looked at me. This guy was not kidding. This wasn't an act. I quit thinking about the time, my uncomfortable chair. Everyone in the room was looking up at him, mesmerized. His voice was pitchy, and he could barely play, but it didn't matter. We believed him. I went from thinking we had nothing in common to taking in his song with respect, even reverence. He sang the final chorus:

> Got holes I can't fill, and bills I can't pay,
> I'm gonna walk in the water 'til my hat floats away

As the last note of the song rang out, there was a long silence. No one moved, we just stared at him. Then, a smattering of applause from the front as a woman stood clapping with tears in her eyes. Somebody in the back stood too. The applause grew louder, and soon the whole room stood. Steve leaned over and said, "That was freaking amazing!"

I desperately wanted to do what the farmer had done. I was traveling a road I wasn't sure of, worried I was too old to be starting this songwriting thing, unsure of my quirky voice and shaky guitar playing. But maybe age, looks, and mastery of my instrument didn't matter as much as I thought they did? The farmer was living proof—what comes from the heart goes to the heart.

His simple song spoke to the innermost part of all of us, and we loved him. In ten years of playing open mics, his was the only standing ovation I ever witnessed. A novice had delivered a song that raised goosebumps on my arms. How did he do it?

When I was a kid, I used to lie in my room in the dark every Friday night and listen to Casey Kasem's American Top 40. It was my favorite radio show, and I'd fight to stay awake for the #1 song of the week, which I'd try to predict in advance. Casey told stories about the songwriters, the bands, and the history of popular music. My nine-year-old eyes would grow heavy, but Casey kept me listening. He'd play the #1 song of the week, then sign off with, "Keep your feet on the ground and keep reaching for the stars."

I was a lonely queer kid in a screwed-up family, and the message I got from my favorite songs was this: I feel as you do, I care about many of the things you care about, and although most people do not seem to care, you are not alone. The difference between thinking nobody on earth got me and at least one person understood was everything to me then. It still is.

Lucinda Williams said in a newspaper interview, "I met a young man who came to me for advice on how to be a good songwriter. I told him don't be afraid to dig into the deepest part of yourself and face your demons. He gave me the saddest look and said, 'I don't think I can do that.' He was afraid to do that. I felt bad for him. It never occurred to me someone would be too afraid to do that."

I was starting to understand. When a songwriter writes what they care about, what truly matters to them, then boils down each line to its essence, the song becomes a snapshot of their soul. These snapshots are infectious; they go out into the world and become a part of the experience of other living souls. The farmer in the hat's song connected us to him, made us know we were not alone.

I'd listened to, leaned on, and loved songs written by Lucinda Williams, Willie Nelson, Bruce Springsteen, Johnny Cash, Woody Guthrie, John Prine, Patti Smith; beloved faces carved in granite on my personal Songwriter's Mount Rushmore. I felt their presence every time I sat down to write. My heroes were iconic, larger than life. I could not imagine myself as that. The farmer inspired me in a new way. He made it seem possible for me to do what he'd done.

Watching him win over the audience with a simple but powerful song gave me permission to sing about what truly mattered to me.

Miles Davis said, "Man, sometimes it takes you a long time to sound like yourself." Yeah, that's what I was struggling with. Sounding like myself. I didn't yet know what that meant. But the instructions the farmer left me with were:

Mean every word.

Sing it simple.

Sing it plain.

Sing it clear.

Sing it true.

Robert Shelton writes in *No Direction Home: The Life and Music of Bob Dylan* that on his first record, Bob Dylan imitated the styles of Dave Van Ronk, Ramblin' Jack Elliot, Eric Von Schmidt, and his hero, Woody Guthrie. I thought, well, if mirroring his heroes for a while was good enough for Dylan, then it was good enough for me too. So, like many beginners, I did the only thing I knew to do. I impersonated my songwriting heroes. I knew I'd have to shed their skin one day, but learning from my heroes through imitation, well, why not?

At my writing desk, guitar in hand, I asked myself, what would Cash do, what would Prine do, what would Guthrie do? Where would Lucinda take this? What would Spring-steen say?

My favorite artists' songs are as identifiable as their faces. They leave fingerprints on their music, a deeply imprinted one-of-a-kind *them*ness, pieces of their DNA, sparks of their spirit. I could identify a Bob Dylan song, a John Prine song, a Bruce Springsteen song, a Woody Guthrie or a Johnny Cash song no matter who sang it.

Up to this point, most of my songs were comprised of one part putting myself out there, two parts trying to sound . . . cool? Smart? Truth was, I agonized over what people thought about me. Was I worthy of people's attention? These worries left many of my songs feeling uninhabited. I had to quit worrying about myself and start making my songwriting about the *song,* not me.

A writer's voice comes through when she expresses her genuine areas of concern: saying here I am, this is what I care about, this is what matters to me. I was not yet sure how to do this, but after I saw the farmer in the hat at the Old Vienna, it was clear I needed to dig deeper and be braver. A few rare souls are born with the ability to create songs in their own voice from the start, but for the rest of us it requires time and effort.

In early days of the AIDS crisis, I saw a billboard on I-10 near New Orleans. In huge red letters, it read:

"AIDS IS GOD'S PUNISHMENT FOR GAYS.
REPENT BEFORE IT IS TOO LATE!"

There was a church's name and number at the bottom. It made me angry, but mostly, it just hurt. I was a bartender at a gay club at the time, and the "gay plague" was all around me. My friends were getting sick, and some were dying.

But in spite of the suffering, "Christian" protestors would show up in a church bus and stand outside the bar with hand-painted signs that said, "God Hates Gays," "RE-PENT Fags!" One night they showed up with a huge cross that they dragged back and forth in front of the bar, shouting, "Jesus died for you! Christ the Lord Saves! Faggots Repent!"

My friend Joey, a DJ at the bar, died of AIDS without the support of his family. His parents abandoned him. My friend Terry and I went to see Joey at Baton Rouge General Hospital, and there were infectious disease warning signs on his door. His room was taped off with DO NOT ENTER yellow crime scene tape. Nurses refused to go in. Food service left his meals on a tray outside the room. Terry decided to get Joey out of there and bring him home to his own apartment to take care of him. A small group of us from the bar took turns caring for Joey at Terry's, till he died. There was no funeral.

I left Baton Rouge and moved to Boston. A year later, Terry was diagnosed with HIV and came to live with me. He died in a Boston hospice the following year. I was with him moments after he passed. I was twenty-eight. He was thirty-three.

Back then, friends lost partners and could not publicly grieve. Their bereavement was not recognized. Some lives were considered to be more worthy of grieving than others, some relationships real and valuable, others dismissed. When a gay man lost his partner, it was as if there was no loss because their relationship was treated as if there was no love. That's the way it was back then.

Sitting at my writing desk a few years after Terry died, I was thinking about him and Joey, the protestors outside the bar, and that God-awful billboard. I wanted to compose a song that spoke to these memories. I was sober at this point and had developed faith in a creator, a mysterious eternal source of constant love and mercy. I dismissed entirely the Old Testament notion of a vengeful God. I believe when we hurt, God hurts. In recovery, we talked about a "higher power." I could not conceptualize this power, but I felt it when love filled the room, when empathy brought us together. Gay men in the meetings were dying. Young, beautiful men, with their entire life ahead of them, stricken by AIDS, came to the recovery meeting using walkers, wheelchairs, canes. They were received with open arms, embraced, asked to speak, and when they died, we all grieved and went to the funeral.

I wanted to work all this into a song, some kind of rebuttal to the hate my friends endured during the early years of the AIDS crisis.

I asked myself, "What had the farmer in the straw hat done to make me believe him? Why did I feel his simple song so deeply?"

Well, for one thing, his song contained pictures, it was like a little movie. The image of a hat floating away as the singer walked deeper and deeper into the water had engaged my imagination, triggered emotion, and seared itself into my being. The farmer could have sung, "She broke my heart, I'm sad and blue, she made me cry, I wanna die," but talking "about" feelings would not have had the same effect.

Preachy proclamations and maudlin statements do not generate empathy.

I could write, "Being cruel to people who are sick and dying is appalling. Homophobia is wrong." But that would suck, just like it would have sucked if the farmer had written, "She broke my heart, I'm sad and blue. She made me cry. I wanna die."

Thinking about the church billboard again, I wrote down, "I don't know what all of this means, I don't think it means what it seems."

This subject mattered to me. I felt it, deep inside. I sang those two lines over the chords Am/F. The melody that came was sad and reflective. I sang it over and over and realized that the "I" in the song was not me, Mary Gauthier. The narrator was a man with the virus, speaking to us from the late eighties. Should I give him a name? I came up with Michael Joe Alexandry (Michael, my brother's name; Joe, my father's name; and Alexandry, my father's mother's maiden name). I had him say, "My name is Michael Joe Alexandry. I been a queer since the day I was born."

Oh, wow, I knew this guy! An unapologetically gay man, he was the voice of friends from the bar who were forced to face an epidemic without the support of their families. It was the voice of all the queers and queens and misfits and allies that I'd known and loved who were abandoned by loved ones when they needed them most. It was also the voice of Michael, my gay waiter who was living with AIDS, who'd brought me to my first twelve-step meeting.

I needed pictures and a story to bring it to life. A little movie. The story started coming, told through the voice of a young man who was doomed and afraid. The voice was an amalgamation of souls I'd loved and lost. I invented the character, but I knew him well. I could tell his story. In fact, I was born to tell this story. My songwriting heroes stood behind my shoulder as I sat at my writing desk. Their guidance was needed, but this story was mine to tell.

When I lived in Baton Rouge, gay bars had no windows. No one wanted to be seen there, and windows would have probably been smashed anyway—maybe even a bomb would have been tossed through them. Gays were hated. Remembering this, I included a downtown bar without windows, where it "always was night."

I thought of a framed photo I had of Terry and me, then pictured Michael Joe Alexandry holding a snapshot of his dead friends, remembering their life before the virus. I saw his mother loving him when he was a child, before she knew he was gay.

"Goddamn HIV" began with my anger about a misguided billboard, then moved into my sorrow for the loss of my friends. I tried to find music on my guitar that matched how I felt. I played chords over and over again, singing words and nonsense sounds until a lyric came through that felt true. I wrote that lyric down and tried to expand the disjointed mess in front of me into something that belonged together, staying focused on the original feeling, using music to expand and deepen it. Every now and then, sparks of inspiration would enter on a current that felt slightly electrical, bringing me a fleeting sensation of connecting to an invisible power source. I sat at my desk for hours and hours, playing chords and singing nonsense, singing what I had. I collected flashes of ideas, riding the edge between what I could see and what was still invisible.

In the last verse, the closing of the movie, I saw Michael on train tracks, walking, alone. A young man with a deadly virus in his blood, looking up at the sky, staring into the infinite black.

Right away, this song felt different.

I felt the influence of my songwriting heroes, but I was not imitating them. The song felt inevitable, like it existed before I ever wrote it. It had an unimpeachable feeling of rightness to it.

"Goddamn HIV" is the first song I wrote that sounds like a Mary Gauthier song. It is the song where, in retrospect, I found my voice. It's written from an outsider's point of view, about a difficult subject, and shines a spotlight on a character rarely heard from, refusing to conform to the demands of the genre it's written in. A song in first person, sung by a gay male narrator dying of AIDS? This was not done in folk or country music. No way. But these elements would become the defining characteristics of what I do.

My search for my voice brought me to the place I had medicated for years, the place where my hurts and fears lay hidden. I was afraid I would be judged, shamed, or even, as irrational as it sounds, somehow annihilated. "Goddamn

HIV" asks me to show my heart. "One does not become enlightened by imagining figures of light," Carl Jung wrote, "but by making the darkness conscious."

To sound like myself, I had to reveal myself. To reveal myself, I had to be brave. I was rising from the ashes of addiction by putting words and melody to the fires that burned inside me. It was not lost on me that the early AIDS activists shouted "silence equals death" as they fought for the medicines they needed. I went there with them, stood in front of the Reagan White House, chanting. I did not know it yet, but by writing my truth, I was writing myself back into the land of the living.

Not that the world took notice. Far from it! What happened, in fact, was pushback. I played "Goddamn HIV" at open mics, and the reaction was mixed. It made some folks uncomfortable. A worried gay man informed me the world had changed, progress had been made, and my song created the wrong impression.

"Why don't you write a happy song about how much better it is now?"

I went on the air at WUMB Folk Radio, and right before turning on the mic, the program director instructed,

"Don't play 'Goddamn HIV.'"

I played it in a feedback session on a Nashville Songwriters Association cruise, and the instructor, a hit songwriter, turned the CD off after the first chorus, flustered. He said, "What the hell do you want me to do with this?"

I played it for a woman who ran a Nashville music conference. She frowned and said it sounded like a "lesbian lament. You should focus your talents on writing songs that are uplifting."

I wanted their approval, of course, but I wasn't going to change the song, no matter what anyone said. Jesus Christ himself could have come down from above to tell me the chorus needed editing, and I would have had to tell him, "I love you Lord, but I'm not touching it." No matter what anyone thought, I knew the song was finished. I had no control over whether people liked it or hated it. It said what my soul needed to say, and I was proud of it. It felt like me somehow, I was *in there*.

Voice contains the mystery of personality. The first few lines of a Dylan song—the tiny passionate brush strokes of a van Gogh painting, the violent redemptive worldview of a Flannery O'Connor story, the spooky cadence of a Poe tale, we immediately recognize these voices. All are universally understood to reflect the spirit of the creator. But what creator am I speaking of? Is it the artist, or the Creator of creativity?

It's both.

Artists hope to tap into the powers from which the masters pull. But the courage it takes to stand alone, speak up first when you are not sure you're right, make mistakes, risk rejection, humiliation, and disdain, combined with the discipline of digging deeper and deeper until the well of truth is finally tapped, well, who is truly interested in that line of work?

Flannery O'Connor said, "Fiction writing is about everything human and we are made out of dust, and if you scorn getting yourself dusty, then you shouldn't try to write fiction. It's not a grand enough job for you."

I'd say the same thing applies to songwriting. When I surrender to its demands, a voice asks me to be a messenger. It comes with instructions on how to use it. Often, the message is disturbing.

Every life contains a massive collection of thoughts and experiences and sensations that are moving at the speed of light and most people never get a chance to just be still and pause and look at them. I was learning to slowly sort out my own voice from the rest of the thoughts, emotions, interpretations, habits, sales pitches, and influences inside me that can overwhelm me at any given moment.

After I wrote "Goddamn HIV," I was left with a deep feeling of certainty, of *rightness*. I'd done my job. Every word, every note, rang true to me. The song contained social commentary about a topic that was very important to me, but the character did not preach. He simply told his story, in his own voice.

My voice.

Three

SAM STONE: PRESCIENCE

Sam Stone

Sam Stone came home to his wife and family
After serving in the conflict overseas
And the time that he served had shattered all his nerves
And left a little shrapnel in his knees

But the morphine eased the pain
And the grass grew round his brain
And gave him all the confidence he lacked
With a purple heart and a monkey on his back

There's a hole in daddy's arm where all the money goes
Jesus Christ died for nothing I suppose
Little pitchers have big ears
Don't stop to count the years
Sweet songs never last too long on broken radios

Sam Stone's welcome home
Didn't last too long
He went to work when he'd spent his last dime
And soon he took to stealing
When he got that empty feeling
For a hundred-dollar habit without overtime

And the gold roared through his veins
Like a thousand railroad trains

And eased his mind in the hours that he chose
While the kids ran around wearing other people's clothes

There's a hole in daddy's arm where all the money goes
Jesus Christ died for nothing I suppose
Little pitchers have big ears
Don't stop to count the years
Sweet songs never last too long on broken radios

Sam Stone was alone
When he popped his last balloon
Climbing walls while sitting in a chair
Well, he played his last request
While the room smelled just like death
With an overdose hovering in the air
But life had lost its fun
There was nothing to be done
But trade his house that he bought on the GI bill,
For a flag-draped casket on a local hero's hill

There's a hole in daddy's arm where all the money goes,
Jesus Christ died for nothing I suppose
Little pitchers have big ears
Don't stop to count the years
Sweet songs never last too long on broken radios

—John Prine

When I was seven, Saturday was my favorite day of the week. The Baton Rouge bookmobile would roll in and park on the boulevard near our house. Mama would walk me there to get in line, and I'd wait my turn to climb on board. Kids were allowed five books. Big decisions, only five books. I'd take my time, make sure my selections were just right. I'd take those books to my bedroom and devour them, then have to wait another five days for the bookmobile to return. Books were my first love, portals to other worlds. They lifted me out of my little room and offered an escape, an entrance to new, exciting adventures. I'd stay in my room, door closed, reading.

My family would watch the *CBS Evening News* every night after supper. Cronkite would open the broadcast by announcing the number of U.S. soldiers lost in the Vietnam War that day, then cut to correspondents reporting from the field in Southeast Asia. He'd sign off with, "And that's the way it is." Cronkite's evening news brought the Vietnam War into our living room for years. The war became very, very real when my cousin Philip was killed in action.

Philip was twenty-three when he died. I was eight. My father, who'd served in Korea, was devastated when he found out we'd lost him. It was the first time I saw my father cry. Philip was the first person I loved who died, and his death haunted me.

We immediately drove from Baton Rouge to Thibodaux when we got the word, directly over to Aunt Dot's, Philip's mom. We kids were told to stay quiet and play outside as adults whispered and wept in the kitchen. The grieving around the kitchen table went on for days as family gathered for Philip's burial.

After the funeral, Aunt Dot framed the American flag from Philip's casket with his medals underneath. She hung it in the hallway next to a framed black-and-white photo of him in uniform. My cousin looked out from behind the glass, his garrison cap slightly tilted on his buzz-cut head: Philip Orgeron, Company A, 2nd Battalion, 60th Infantry, 9th Infantry Division, Army-PFC-E3, killed in action, in Tây Ninh, Vietnam. When I think of him now, I see that picture.

Things at home were becoming increasingly volatile. My parents were fighting nightly, and the battles were escalating. They both became increasingly suicidal. In the heat of their fights, my father, drunk after seven or eight martinis, would pull his belt out of his pants, put it around his neck, and storm around the house, drunk, looking for a place to hook it.

One Saturday morning, I woke up to window-rattling thunder. A fast-moving thunderstorm was blowing through, rolling up angry and black from the Gulf of Mexico. Lightning flashed, lights flickered, thunder exploded. Rain bounced off my bedroom window, pinging the glass like thousands of tiny rocks. As the wind howled, I heard my parents shouting. Another terrible fight.

I threw my robe on and ran to them. As I entered the kitchen, Daddy was forcing open a bottle of Librium. He poured a pile of pills into his hand, and I knocked them out. As they scattered on the kitchen floor, I thought Mama might be making a move for the knife drawer, so I instinctively blocked it. We were screaming at the top of our voices as rain blew in furious sheets across our concrete driveway.

My little brother and sister were sitting at the kitchen table in their pajamas, waiting for breakfast, terrified, crying. I can't remember how it ended, but somehow, like all the other times, life went on.

My parents' fighting continued. The police came to our door several times in response to my mother's frantic calls. At some point, I gave up trying to understand my parents' war, the Vietnam War, my own war with my father. Something deep inside began to crystalize. I became pissed off, defiant. I stayed in my room when I heard my parents yelling, locked my door, put my headphones on, turned the music up. Got high.

We lived in a Baton Rouge subdivision called Tara. Hundreds of cookie-cutter houses with manicured lawns and two American-made cars in covered carports. The neighborhood streets were deserted after midnight, houses stayed dark till dawn. I began sneaking out after my parents went to bed. My neighborhood friends would tap on my window and I'd climb out and be off into the night, exhilarated with freedom. Walking the empty streets with my new friends felt like being released from jail.

We'd search for unlocked cars parked on the street, stealing anything of value we might be able to use. I brought my dad's blue Pan Am airplane carry-on bag with me to put the loot in and wore gloves to prevent fingerprints, like on TV.

It felt like a game.

One night, without much thought, we stole a car. The owner had left the keys in the ignition, and the oldest girl in our group jumped in the driver's seat and said, "Let's go!" I figured we were going to ride around for a while and bring it back, but my friends decided to keep the car and run away from home.

It was more than I bargained for, and I got scared. I asked them to bring me home and drop me off at the end of my parents' driveway. I stood alone in the early morning darkness and watched them drive away, climbed back into my bedroom window, sat on my bed, and cried. Trouble was coming.

The next week my mother decided to leave my father. She filed for divorce and quickly moved me and my brother and sister to my grandparents' house in Thibodaux. I don't know how she knew, but I think my fast-blooming delinquency gave her the final push out of her failed marriage. Not long after, my friends who'd run away from home were arrested for grand theft auto in the car we'd stolen.

While I struggled to adjust to a new town and a new school, my friends were in juvenile jail, a dreadful place outside Baton Rouge called Louisiana Training Institute

(LTI); the facilities did not meet legal standards and it was eventually shut down. I felt guilty for having dodged arrest and was worried sick about my friends.

I started skipping class and getting high with guys I'd meet at Peltier Park, the local stoner hang. I was sitting alone under a tree in the park one morning when a car pulled over and the driver said "hi." I did not know him, but I got in. We got high, and when the dope was gone, he said we could get more, but we'd have to go to an apartment in the worst part of town, where there had been a shooting the week before.

He said, "Look, you need to know the dealer's apartment is awful. People are crammed inside there, sitting in the dark, wasted. The place is filthy, it reeks. I think I can score, but maybe you should wait in the car." He checked my face for a reaction.

I looked over at him.

He was embarrassed, worried about where he was taking me. He looked down, his sandy brown curls soft against the sides of his skinny freckled cheeks, both hands held tight on the wheel. He'd accepted whatever world was inside that apartment as his fate, but in an act of kindness that still moves me, he was protective of me, as if I was worth protecting.

I pretended to consider what he had said, but I knew what I wanted. I was going in.

We drove to the dealer's apartment, knocked on the door.

A man answered. We stepped inside. I hesitated in the hallway. The smell of stale cigarette smoke, weed, and rotting garbage filled my nose. It was disturbingly dark.

My new friend said, "You wait here, ok? I'll be back."

The living room had a single black light. Several psychedelic black light posters glowed on the walls. As my eyes adjusted, I could see people crammed on the couch, on beanbag chairs, on the floor, everywhere. Stoned wasted, heads rolling downward. Cigarettes glowed. Filthy ashtrays spilled over, smoldered. Empty beer bottles and sticky soda cans sitting on every table and countertop, bags of trash overflowed along the wall. Windows covered in duct-taped tinfoil, no light could get in. I stayed in the hallway, afraid to enter.

No one looked over at me.

Someone dropped a needle on a record. I listened from where I stood. The singer seemed like a nice man.

It was John Prine singing "Sam Stone."

The song landed on my ears like a dream partially remembered and flooded me with foreboding. Like some kind of a warning. I was in a vortex, pulled along by the song, a hallway marionette. Everything began to feel inevitable. The word "morphine" grabbed me. "Easing the pain" was what morphine did for Sam Stone. Easing the pain, yes, that got my attention.

Sam Stone's drug habit was sucking the life out of him, while his "kids ran around wearing other people's clothes." I felt bad for the guy in the song. But I felt worse because of something inside me, something I didn't understand. The song ended. Where the hell was my new friend? I wanted the dope, and I wanted to get out of there.

How could I have felt the visceral, magnetic pull of my own future in a fictional song about a traumatized Vietnam veteran? What was this foreknowledge?

Prescience. Pre-science.

Prescience is the foretelling of things before they exist or happen. It's the province of timeless art, and the mainstay of songs that endure. A prescient song continues to be relevant in new ways over time. Like fine wine or whiskey, timeless songs become even *more* true as the winds of change blow.

"Sam Stone" opens with simple sustained organ chords, the sound of a funeral hymn. Sad and rustic, the tone captures the universal essence of grief, a somber, lonesome tone I imagine spilling out of an old country church. John Prine enters, a minister addressing his congregation gathered there to mourn. His voice is matter-of-fact, telling a story that must be told. A lullaby of loss.

John's thumb plays alternating base notes on the guitar, steady, relentless, pushing the story forward. His world-weary voice sings of a battle lost, a soldier lost, and a war lost.

Listening to "Sam Stone" was like looking into a murky mirror. I couldn't stop staring. I bought John's first record and played it over and over again. I'd lift the needle off the record when "Sam Stone" was done, place it back down, and listen again.

My troubles with drugs and alcohol were in their early stages, but my addiction was a beast from day one. I was young, but I'd been through plenty. "Sam Stone" was one of the first songs I learned to play on my guitar, by heart, words and music. The song was not like the songs on the radio, it was too real, too true, too sad. It was better than those songs, a lot better.

I loved it.

I moved back to Baton Rouge, and on Friday afternoons my roommates would meet at the Brass Rail Bar for happy hour after their classes at Louisiana State University let out for the week. The Rail offered shots of whiskey for thirty-five cents, three till seven o'clock, all you could drink, every Friday. Long lines formed as LSU students converged and bikers rolled in after work. By early afternoon, the beer garden was overflowing with drunks swirling in and out, bouncing off one another. The roar of the music made everybody shout.

The Rail accommodated the Friday throngs by throwing sheets of plywood over sawhorses, then having the bartender line up rows and rows of plastic cups and pour rotgut bourbon over them, shot after shot, hour after hour. Students and bikers would sit at picnic tables under green Heineken umbrellas, drinking, smoking cigarettes, and talking.

Rowdy drunken college kids bumping into bikers sometimes led to trouble. There were brawls, but mostly we got along. Sooner or later someone would show up with weed, and we'd go to the parking lot and stand around my mother's old Buick station wagon and get high. I'd put the tailgate down, pull out my guitar, and hand it to anyone willing to play. I'd eventually play a few songs too. I loved it when everyone sang along. The group singing would draw more bikers, their boots crunching in the gravel parking lot, as an unlikely mix of drunks of all ages, sexual preferences, and political views stood around the tailgate of the station wagon.

Bikers, most of them only a few years out of Vietnam, would ask me for John Prine songs. Grizzly, a three-hundred-pound biker, wanted to hear "Sam Stone." He'd get teary-eyed by the first chorus, slam a shot of cheap bourbon, crush the plastic cup, tilt his head skyward, and shout,

"FUCKIN HELL GOTDAMNIT HELL FUCKIN YEA BABY!"

He'd wrap me in a bear hug and spin me in the air when the song ended and say, "Darlin', PLAY IT AGAIN."

So, I would.

There's a hole in daddy's arm where all the money goes
Jesus Christ died for nothing I suppose

Griz would stomp through the parking lot gravel back to the bar to order more drinks for all of us, his broad shoulders swaying, as the silver chain from his wallet rubbed against the huge leg of his washed-out Levi's. I loved how singing "Sam Stone" for Griz made me feel. The same song that made a three-hundred-pound former Marine weep also spoke deeply to a seventeen-year-old gay girl who'd been through a different kind of war.

Not too long after this, I overdosed, and my roommate, an emergency room nurse, could not resuscitate me. He called an ambulance, the paramedics worked on me, and I narrowly escaped death. Sam Stone and I were beginning to look a lot alike.

John Prine said he called his vet Sam Stone, made up the name, because it rhymed with "home." He was twenty-four years old when he wrote it. He created the character as a composite from three or four veteran friends after he got home from the service.

"I had this picture in my mind of a little girl, like Little Orphan Annie, shaking her head back and forth while a rainbow of money goes into her dad's arm. I think I invented the character of Sam Stone as a story line just to get around to that chorus."

John Prine never imagined the song would become one of the greatest anti-war songs of all time, relevant fifty years after he wrote it. Prescience is in the song, more than the songwriter.

And I never imagined that while writing this chapter on my greatest songwriting hero, he'd slip out of this life in a pandemic and we'd lose him to Covid-19. For the ten days he was in a hospital on a respirator, it was all I could think about. I prayed, I hoped, I waited, and I checked his wife Fiona's social feed hourly. When John passed, I sat down on the side of my bed, put my head in my hands, and wept.

The sage-like prophecy of this song pointed to what I would become before I became it. It had a profound influence on me as a songwriter, was my greatest teacher. "Sam Stone" was my guiding light, my North Star, when I was invited to co-write songs with wounded veterans. More on that later, but this song remains my go-to song when I need guidance on how to tell a hard story with precision, emotional honesty, and empathy. "Sam Stone" is tattooed on my soul.

John Prine abides.

Four

DRAG QUEENS IN LIMOUSINES: STORY/MEANING

Drag Queens in Limousines

I Hated High school, prayed it would end
The jocks and their girls, it was their world I didn't fit in
Mama said, "Baby, it's the best school that money can buy,
Hold your head up, be strong, c'mon Mary, try."

I stole mama's car on a Sunday and left home for good,
Moved in with my friends in the city, in a bad neighborhood.
Charles was a dancer, he loved the ballet,
And Kimmy sold pot and read Kerouac and Hemingway.

Drag Queens in Limousines nuns in blue jeans
Dreamers with big dreams all took me in

Charly and I flipped burgers to cover the rent
And Bourbons at Happy hour for .35 cents
One day before work we got drunk and danced in the rain
They fired us both, said, "Don't y'all come back here again."

Drag Queens in Limousines nuns in blue jeans
Dreamers with big dreams all took me in

My dad went to college, and he worked for the state
He never quit nothing he wanted me to graduate
My brother and sister both play in the marching band
They tell me they miss me, but I know they don't understand.

Sometimes you've got do, what you've got to do
And hope that the people you love, will catch up with you

Yea Drag Queens in Limousines nuns in blue jeans
Dreamers with big dreams poets and AWOL marines
Actors and Bar Flies writers with Dark Eyes
Drunks that Philosophize these are my friends

—Mary Gauthier and Crit Harmon

After I got sober, I stayed on the couch for weeks, watching the Persian Gulf War on TV. My face felt pressed against a Mt. Everest of problems. I was twenty-eight but wondered if I had enough time left in my life to deal with the wreckage I was facing. My life was a mess. For weeks I stared transfixed at the visuals shot on a night-vision camera that painted cities in luminous green with a black background, tracer bullets arcing like endless streams of deadly shooting stars streaking over blackened skies.

But in spite of how defeated I felt, I willingly went to the court-mandated recovery meetings three times a week. When asked to speak, I spoke. At a year sober I was asked to tell my story in front of the group. They said, "Tell us what you have been through. It will show us what we can survive." So, I spoke about what had happened: my parents' fights, my eighteenth birthday in jail, my overdose, my drunk driving arrest, being bailed out by my former girlfriend who showed up in full leather in a car I co-signed for, with her new girlfriend, who was also in full leather, a dominatrix. Apparently, I'd interrupted their work. When I shared that little tidbit, the room burst into laughter. I was stunned, then realized this shit is kinda funny. As I spoke, meeting after meeting, I was starting to see a pattern. After I told my story, people said they got something from my experiences, something *they* needed. It surprised me. The feeling of being useful brought hope. It's healing to be heard, to be a part of a group that understands you. I had no idea, but looking back now, I can see I was trying to construct a narrative to make some kind of sense out of what had happened to me.

Woody Guthrie said, "The note of hope is the only note that can help us or save us from falling to the bottom of the heap of evolution, because, largely, about all a human being is, anyway, is just a hoping machine." I wholeheartedly agree and would add that we are also meaning-making machines, and what we have to help us make meaning is our stories.

In recovery meetings, we are told to speak of our "experience, strength, and hope." I was learning how to arrange what seemed like unrelated events into a *story*. A story that *made sense* in some kind of fundamental way. I was powerless over booze and dope, but I was not powerless over how I told my story or how my story ends. It was the stories that kept me in the recovery rooms after my court-ordered visits expired. So many amazing stories.

I started writing songs a few years after I emerged from the wreckage of addiction. In retrospect, I believe my songs served as stepping stones to a new life. My songs, like me sharing my story, helped me find purpose in the pain. I was starting to see even the worst things that happened to me could help others.

This was a revelation.

I attended a songwriting workshop with the American Society of Composers, Authors and Publishers (ASCAP) artist rep, songwriter, and song publisher Ralph Murphy. In the workshop, Ralph said, "The basic profile of a songwriter is a monumentally dysfunctional human being with a host of problems, who comes from an equally dysfunctional family, some of which have been scarred by addiction, violence, mental illness, murders or suicides or both. Our profile is physically, sexually, emotionally abused, orphaned or from a broken home." I laughed. So did everyone else.

Ralph jokingly said, "If you have an acute inability to communicate on a personal level, and you're truly bad at relationships yet live with an overwhelming desperate, desperate, need to be loved, you might one day be a candidate for the songwriters Hall of Fame." By then, I'd told my story often enough to recognize myself in this description, and I was thrilled. I'd found my people! Ralph said our wounds are what can make us great. I knew I had an advantage here. I had a treasure chest of wounds.

Ralph encouraged us to remember why we loved our favorite songs. He said, "You loved them because they gave you, you. They seemed to touch some deep nerve in you. You've lived this. You've felt it. In other words, it's not your job to sing the listeners your diary. Your job is to sing the listeners *theirs*." Ralph told us that Joni Mitchell said if you see her instead of yourself in her music, the song is irrelevant. I listened closely, took notes, and wondered how, exactly, is that done?

For many years, booze and dope were how I dealt with discomfort. Getting high brought relief, calmed the anxious beast inside me. I would drink before I went out drinking because I needed relief from my dis-ease. It worked, for a while. But it ended up making my life worse. So, I ended up drinking even more and using stronger doses of drugs to make *that* discomfort go away. Then the real pain started. I spent fifteen years in a downward spiral. I ended up terribly disconnected, removed, isolated, and lonely.

I went to my first rehab when I was fifteen and spent my sixteenth birthday there, in lockdown. I got out, relapsed, went back, and was sent to a halfway house in Kansas.

While I was at the halfway house I got a job working at a Salina car wash in the dead of the Kansas winter. My job at the car wash was simple. I sprayed ice and snow off of cars, removing salt and sand, then drove them through the wash. One day, a police officer came in and asked for the owner. I pointed him to the door of Big Jim's office. He walked in and closed the door behind him. A few minutes later he came out with Big Jim by his side. Big Jim told all three of us employees to come to the detail room.

He said, "There was a theft from a car driven through the car wash today. I have to ask you all to stand against the wall." Big Jim spoke softly, his long face and big round eyes looking *very* concerned.

Red lined up, back against the wall, staring straight ahead, refusing to make eye contact. In his late fifties, his chiseled, clean-shaven, pox-marked face was rugged and handsome, with a look of disdain around the edges of his mouth. In the sleeve of his yellowed Fruit of the Loom t-shirt, rolled up above his tattooed biceps, he always kept a pack of Marlboro Reds, which is where he got his nickname. His job was to wax and buff cars in the detail room. It was the best job at the car wash because there was a floor heater in there.

Red hated cops.

He glanced at me as I stood next to him against the wall. His body language said *don't worry kid, I got your back.* We'd been smoking weed before work every day. He was my friend.

Silas was the oldest of the three of us. Wide-set, blood-shot eyes; short gray hairs sticking out both sides of his head from beneath his battered Vietnam-era military cap; heavy bellied, shirt untucked. He looked down. His slouched demeanor read "innocent of all charges, sir, too weary to steal jack shit from anyone." Silas drank daily, all day long. He probably had a half pint of vodka in his boot at the moment.

The cop said again, "Listen, one of you stole a bottle of prescription pills out of a car this morning. The three of you are going to stand there until one of you comes forward and admits it."

I stood terrified, looked out the window at the snow spilling from the sad gray sky. I'd never lived where there was snow before. My tennis shoes were wet, my toes numb, my feet freezing. I could not afford waterproof snow boots on the $2.10 an hour the car wash paid.

Some of the women at the halfway house worked as hotel maids and made decent tips, but I was not going to wear a blue, tightfitting maid's dress. No way. Two women at the house worked at Tony's pizza factory for $7.10 an hour, the highest-paying job, but you needed a car to get there and had to be eighteen to apply. I was seventeen with no car.

I could walk to the car wash. I needed this job. If I lost it, I'd get thrown out of the halfway house. I'd be homeless. I'd saved up around sixty bucks, but that wouldn't get me far.

I tried to look innocent. Tried to look young. Tried to look like anything but what I was: a seventeen-year-old thief in a police lineup.

I stood shivering next to Silas and Red with two stolen 8-track tapes in each boot, a bottle of stolen phenobarbital in my left pocket, and a couple bucks' worth of coins in my other pocket—all stolen. I'd also grabbed a nice pair of lined leather gloves this morning. They were in my coat pocket in the break room. The cop stared in silence. Big Jim's long face remained deeply concerned. Silas and Red looked straight ahead.

The pressure was too much. I buckled.

"It was me. I did it." I pulled the bottle of phenobarbital out of my pocket and gave it to the cop.

Red shook his head, then gazed out the window.

Silas's face was blank.

Big Jim breathed a sigh of relief.

The cop took the pills from my hand, pulled the cuffs off his belt, told me to put my hands behind my back, and snapped the cuffs onto my wrists. He thanked Silas and Red, shook hands with Big Jim, whose concerned look disappeared now that the cop was leaving his car wash.

The cop walked me out to his car. The temperature was

in single digits, and swirling sheets of snow were blowing and piling up on top of the plowed, frozen, brown snow along the sides of the building.

The cop opened the back door of his police car, took the cuffs off my wrists, and told me to get in. He got into the driver's seat, turned the engine on, and blasted the heat as I sat shivering in the back seat, wondering how to get the stolen 8-track tapes out of my sports socks.

He put his right arm on top of his seat, looked at me in his rearview mirror, turned his head. "Listen," then spoke in a dad's voice, "I don't want to arrest you. But you stole those pills from a priest's car, a monsignor. The best I can do is call and ask Monsignor if he wants to press charges, given the circumstances. Those guys you're working with, they're too old for you. It's not good for a young girl like you to be spending so much time with old men. I know a nice lady with a little café in town. Maybe I can get you a waitress job there. But for now, I've got to bring you in. Here's my card, call me when you get out."

I nodded. "Thank you, sir."

Before we got to the Salina county jail I managed to get the 8-tracks out of my sports socks and kick them under his seat.

At the jail, a cop took my fingerprints, emptied my pockets, booked me, and walked me down the hall into a solitary cell: twelve by twelve, steel walls, steel toilet, steel bunk, thin mattress, no pillows, and no windows. Single yellow light bulb in a cage on the ceiling. The cell door closed, and I panicked.

I lay down, I paced, I sat. I stood. Over and over again.

No sounds, no smells, nothing to see, nothing to do. I sat on the steel bench, wrapped my arms around myself, and rocked. No idea of time, of day or night. After hours of rocking and pacing, I finally wept. Then I slept.

I woke in terror. No clock, no time, a silent, empty room.

What was probably very early the next morning, keys jangled; the cell door opened. I'd never been so happy to see anyone in my life. A church lady entered. The woman's clothes looked like she'd walked out of an episode of *Little House on the Prairie*. A brown dress with a black apron, both tied tight at the waist. Black shoes, flats, with black laces, and a bonnet, made of the same material as the dress. No matter, all good. Her old-timey look was perfect. Laura Ingalls, I love you!

She was plain spoken and plain dressed. I didn't know her religion nor did I care. I just kept saying "THANK GOD you are here. THANK GOD you are here." She sat next to me on the thin mattress on the hard steel bunk and pulled her Bible out of an old leather shoulder bag. She read Bible verses, then asked me if I wanted to sing. I nodded my head yes, let's sing. We sang "Amazing Grace" together. When she got up to leave, I begged her to stay. She refused but promised she'd be back the following week. I nodded but did not answer. I could not imagine being in a cage that long. Before she left, I asked what the date was. She said it was March 11, 1980.

It was my eighteenth birthday.

Early on in my troubadour travels, I was asked to play a half-baked gig in NYC, one that ended before it began. When it became clear that no one was coming, and the gig was a bust, my friends offered to take me out to their favorite greasy spoon, the Midtown Diner, near Times Square.

The diner had a parking lot that horseshoed around the front and sides of the building. The spots were filled with limos and black sedans. Impressive—all those fancy cars lined up, engines running, chauffeurs inside drinking coffee, some of them eating out of takeout boxes, waiting for their next job. My friends said the diner let them hang there between fares if they bought something to eat.

We were seated in a booth and given menus. I sank into a bit of a funk. As I sat brooding, a door swung open in the back of the room and two drag queens in full makeup, high heels, sparkly dresses, and big, big hair strutted in and ordered coffee to go. They stood at the counter waiting, talking loudly, gesticulating, and laughing in that loud drag queen "look-at-me" tone.

I stared, but the staff and customers didn't even turn their heads. Apparently, they were aware of the bar next door. The queens were now runway walking through the restaurant and back through the swinging doors. Styrofoam cups in hand, they left the sweet smell of their perfume behind them as they disappeared into what appeared to be a drag bar connected to the diner. I could hear the music kick on, the thumping of the bass, and some queen singing on stage. I looked at my friends in amazement, laughed, and said, "C'mon guys, isn't this a little surreal?"

My friends smiled and said, "We love this place! Drag

queens and limousines!" When they said that, I was flooded with scenes from my past and a gut feeling. I wrote those words down on a napkin, folded it, and put it in my pocket, saving it for later.

Then, I ordered dinner.

I was released from the Kansas jail the day after my eighteenth birthday under the condition I leave the state and never return. I moved back home with my mother and ended up driving her car to Baton Rouge without her permission and moving in with my old friends. I kept the car, an old Buick station wagon, and landed a minimum-wage restaurant job with my friend Tom.

On Friday afternoons we'd get stupid drunk at happy hour at The Brass Rail, then work the dinner shift at the Tiger Town Mr. Gatti's Pizza. I was a cashier. Tom manned the ovens.

Tom would burn the hairs off his arms when the dinner rush came, sometimes searing his flesh as well. From the register I could hear him yelling, "Fuck! Ouch! Shit!" I'd race through transactions, hit zeros when I thought no one was looking, and grab as much cash from the drawer as I thought I could get away with stealing. I thought of it as party money and shared the booze and weed with my friends.

We were fired.

We ended up as dishwashers at a college burger joint called Round the Corner Restaurant. Round the Corner (RTC) had red phones on the tables. When you lifted the receivers, they lit up a switchboard in the kitchen, and an operator answered. On LSU football game nights, the restaurant filled to capacity. The entire switchboard would light up bright red. Frat boys saw the phones as an opportunity to be comedians, ordering things like "Two fur burgers with extra cum juice." Frat boys aside, the phones eliminated the need for waitresses and solved the problem of long lines at the counter. We'd buzz the table from the switchboard when the food was ready, and the customer would come to the counter, pay, and take their tray of food to their table. This is where I met Kenny, a coaching assistant for the LSU football team.

Kenny ate at RTC nightly. One of his legs was smaller than the other, shriveled and shrunken from a birth defect. The foot on the affected leg was also twisted outward. He more or less dragged it behind him. Kenny would strike up long conversations with me at the counter while he slowly paid for his burger and beer. Sometimes he'd come in at closing time and we'd talk. Kenny's earnest smile was sweet. I grew to like him. A new friend, I thought. He was not flirting, not creepy. Mostly, he was like a little brother, a guy who needed looking after.

He began suggesting that we go to New Orleans together on a Saturday night and "have us some fun." He didn't own a car, but he knew I had my mother's old station wagon. After casually talking about it for months, I started to seriously consider it.

I was born in New Orleans, but I lived there only as an infant. At about a year old, I was adopted from St. Vincent's orphanage and moved to Baton Rouge. I'd return to New

Orleans with my Italian immigrant adoptive grandparents for monthly pilgrimages to their beloved Central Grocery to load up on Italian meats, cheeses, olive oil, cookies, and muffalettas. My grandfather would put the haul in an Igloo ice chest and bring it back home to Thibodaux for us to share.

My adult idea of New Orleans certainly contained some vague notion of distant and forbidden fun. The more Kenny talked about showing me his favorite bar, the more the idea grew on me. So, late one Sunday afternoon we took off for New Orleans, headed for the French Quarter. I drove, Kenny directed, "Take I-10 East from Baton Rouge to New Orleans. Exit on Vieux Carre, then three turns later we're there. The Midship Bar, on Iberville Street."

We made it to the French Quarter without a problem and parked a few blocks away. As we walked the cobblestone streets and approached the Midship Bar, I noticed a steady line of cars circling the block. Drivers were slowing down in front of the bar, and ladies in short skirts walked up to the rolled-down passenger windows. They pressed their hips against the sides of cars, laughing and flirting with the drivers, skirts riding up the back of their legs, fishnet stockings exposed, sparkly high heels glittering under the streetlights. Some would hop into the passenger side and ride off, or the car would move on. Then another car would slowly come around, and the process would repeat.

I had no way of knowing that ten years prior, on another Sunday evening in June 1973, one of the deadliest crimes against gays and lesbians in the history of the United States had occurred next door, at the UpStairs Lounge, where an arsonist set the gay bar on fire, killing thirty-two people and injuring many more. Media reports and the police response to the fire were less than sympathetic. Some family members of the deceased refused to claim the ashes of their loved ones. Radio commentators joked the remains should be buried in fruit jars. On the issue of identifying the victims, the New Orleans Police Department said, "We don't even know if the papers belonged to the bodies we found them on. Thieves hung out there, and you know this was a queer bar." (At the time, many gay men routinely carried false identification to gay bars in order to avoid being outed in the newspapers in the event they were arrested during a police raid.)

The media coverage was cruel and the police response nonchalant, but the religious establishment's reaction was downright hateful. Church after church refused the use of their facilities for a memorial service. Father Richardson at St. George's Episcopal Church, however, believed the dead should have a service and, over the protest of many parishioners, officiated a prayer service in St. George's sanctuary. He received hate mail from parishioners and massive blowback from people in the community at large. Like so much of the city of New Orleans, this street Kenny and I were walking was haunted.

We made our way along the busy sidewalk, through the hustle and bustle of the women and the cars, and entered the Midship Bar. Kenny, still wearing his aviator Ray-Bans in spite of how dark the bar was, ordered a shot of bourbon and a beer from the tall, sexy bleached-blond bartender. She put a napkin in front of me. I pointed at what Kenny ordered and said, "Same."

I was in a black tailored men's button-down shirt, a black leather biker's vest, black jeans, a chained Harley wallet, and charcoal Justin biker boots. People had confused me for a boy since I was ten. In the past, it was embarrassing, but tonight I was glad my gender was hidden. I felt safer here as a man.

Kenny, on the other hand, looked like Howdy Doody in shades. His gray sweatpants sagged in the crotch and hung so low his butt crack showed. As always, his white sports socks with red stripes were pulled up to his knees over the bottom of his sweatpants. He completed the outfit with an LSU sweatshirt, his favorite number—34—on it, and an LSU baseball cap worn backward to cover his receding hairline. We were quite the couple.

As I scanned the room, Kenny leaned over and whispered, "Stay here, don't go anywhere, I'll be back."

I didn't see him again for three hours.

I stood at the bar sipping my bourbon and beer. Waiting. After a while, I ordered another round and took a closer look at the bartender. She was tall, a good 6'2" or so, and thin. She had a large shock of blond hair pinned in an updo that fell down dramatically across her exposed milky shoulders. She had high prominent cheekbones, a sturdy square chin, rings on all her fingers, and long manicured crimson fingernails. Her wrists were loaded with silver bracelets that jangled as she poured drinks and ran the

register. Her low-cut top fell off her shoulders, drawing
attention to her perfectly shaped breasts. She sashayed as
she worked, hips moving in time to the loud music. I tried
to make small talk with her.

"So, hi, what's your name?"

"Glenda."

"Ahh, yes, Glenda, the good witch?"

"Oh honey," she said, instantly exasperated. "Yes. The
fucking good witch."

"So Glenda, you like working here?"

She paused.

Looked me up and down.

I guess I passed inspection, because she softened. "I
work here in between surgeries. This job pays my bills. I
fly back and forth to Stockholm as often as I can. I'm in the
process of a sex change."

I'd never met anyone who'd had a sex change. My first
thought blurted out of my mouth.

"Wow, that's amazing! Does it hurt?"

"Honey, being born the wrong sex hurts more than any
surgery ever could."

"Yea, yea. Damn. Are the other girls here having sex
changes too?"

"No, it's too expensive for most of them. They live their
lives as women but cannot afford the surgical transition.
Most of them would, if they could."

"How much does one of those operations cost?"

"The price varies from doctor to doctor. I am in it for
about $50,000 so far. I've been taking the hormones for

a year now. My top is fully done." She patted her perfect breasts and strutted off to take a drink order from another customer.

I looked around the room again. Reality check. Every woman in this bar was in various stages of cross-dressing or gender reassignment. Most of them looked like women to me, flashy but feminine, and sexy. I was the only woman in the bar born with a vagina, and I looked like a man.

Kenny had left me to fend for myself in a cross-dresser, transsexual bordello populated by complex New Orleans ladies of the night.

I sat waiting. Watching, pretending to be masculine, tough. Made more small talk with Glenda, had a few more drinks as the working women came and went. Nobody bothered me, but I sat at the bar alone wondering why I was here.

Yet, when Kenny got back, I said nothing. Neither did he. We drove home in silence. I never said a word to him or anyone else about that night.

"Drag Queens in Limousines" was born out of these experiences. I wrote it in the early years of my recovery. This song spends five minutes forty seconds placing the narrator on a hero's journey, pointing to their courage, romanticizing fellow misfits, and making victors out of outsiders and outlaws. It's a high five to those who, like me, feel as though they don't fit in. I had no idea people all over the world would relate, but they did.

In Maynooth, Ontario, a sweet, gray-haired man came

up to me after the show and said, "Mary, you are doing this for all of us. Trans and queer kids, as well as guys like me, a sixty-five-year-old man molested for eight years by a pedophile priest." In Texas, cowboys sang along to the chorus, smiling. In Santa Cruz, old hippies swayed to this song, hands in the air as they danced. In Scotland, middle-aged lorry drivers triumphantly pumped their fists to the bridge:

Sometimes you've got do, what you've got to do
And pray that the people you love, will catch up with you

Clarity comes from stories. They help us make sense of our lives. Witnessing other people's lives through stories is a kind of medicine, and the magic is in getting the story emotionally honest.

Guy Clark once said, "We're all pretty much living the same life just hitting the marks at different times." "Drag Queens in Limousines" showed me that I have no idea what's going on inside a person's heart, in that tender place that the poet Miller Williams, Lucinda's father, described as, "Where the spirit meets the bone." Until I wrote this song and played it for people, I had no idea most everyone has felt like an outsider at some point in their life, but they have.

That outsider feeling is universal.

Five

OUR LADY OF THE SHOOTING STARS: PARADOX AND MYSTERY

Our Lady of the Shooting Stars

Our lady of the shooting stars was that you last night?
Did we dance a whispered waltz did I hold you in my sight?
When morning came with open arm and lifted you
*   from me,*
Sunlight burned my eyes away and now I cannot see.

Our lady of the shooting stars, as I face the early light
All that I can think of now is joining you in flight
But I have followed gypsies girl lost my way back home
Held the phoenix to my chest and ended up alone.

If I move to you will you move to me?
If I move to you will you move to me?

Our lady of the shooting stars, teach me how to know
I want to feel my thoughts go dark and rest inside your flow.
I'll awaken without fear and breathe the cool clean air,
Your words upon my lips your will is my prayer

If I move to you will you move to me?
If I move to you will you move to me?

Our lady of the shooting stars, look what you have done
You led me to the water's edge running from sun.

Are you in the briny mist do Seagulls scream your name?
Wings suspended by your love, or do I reach in vain?

If I move to you will you move to me?
If I move to you will you move to me?

—Mary Gauthier

Back when I was playing open mics and dreaming of the day I'd play my own shows, I was invited to open for a friend at the legendary Wintertide Coffeehouse on Martha's Vineyard. It was one of my first opportunities to play an opening slot, and I was excited. I rode the ferry to the Vineyard with a small overnight bag, thirty copies of my first CD, and my guitar. I was thinking my ship had finally come in. My music career had begun!

But no one came to the show.

Not one person.

I wanted to just go back home and hide, but there were no boats out till morning. I could not slip out the back door and pretend this wasn't happening. My friend said, "What the hell, let's just play." So we did. We performed for each other, the sound man, the bartender, and a room full of empty chairs.

The experience unnerved me. I was successful in the restaurant business. I had a condo, health insurance, and a brand-new leased truck every two years. I had job security and plenty of freedom, but I did not enjoy the daily complexities of employing so many people. The thought of making my living with a guitar, a bar stool, and a spotlight was very, very appealing. I was called to music, but what if I was delusional? If I failed, there'd be plenty of people who'd say I told you so. My business partners laughed out loud when I told them I was starting to take songwriting seriously.

I understood their concern. I was new to the business of music, but I'd already seen lots of people, level-headed in other areas of their lives, who behaved a little kookily when it came to their music. I'd spent many, many nights at open mics listening to some pretty bad music delivered with passion. As I stood on stage and stared at the empty chairs in the Wintertide Coffeehouse that night, I was asking myself, was I one of them? Playing to no one while fighting a deep sense of unworthiness and shame made for one of the longest thirty minutes on stage of my entire career.

The early years are hard for songwriters who play their own songs. No fans. No press. No money. No idea if you have what it takes. I'd seen gifted songwriters who never got much, if any, external validation. They did their work in earnest and committed to their calling, living in obscurity, working day jobs, playing open mics and small bar gigs when they could get them. Others formed cover bands and snuck in originals every now and then, hoping to one day get traction as songwriters. I did not have the time to go those routes. I needed to work my way into the small folk listening rooms, build a little following, and figure out how to grow it. After that night at the Wintertide, I began to wonder, maybe I should just stay in the restaurant business and find a way to love it again or look for happiness some other way? Faceplanting at my first coffeehouse gig was an ominous sign of where I might be headed.

On the ferry home the next morning, I leaned on the boat railing and stared at the churn of saltwater behind the boat as we left Vineyard Haven. The early morning sun warmed my face and hundreds of gulls gathered around us as we made our way out into the bay. The birds hovered close to the boat as passengers tossed them scraps of muffins and donuts that they devoured with enthusiasm, squawking, crooning, squealing, and cooing. Mesmerized, I stared as they soared and dove without flapping their wings. As we made our way out into open waters, surprisingly, they stayed with us, riding the boat wind all the way back to Buzzards Bay.

After I got home, I sat at my writing desk, feeling the sting of my failed gig. I remembered how excited I was on the ferry ride over and how defeated I felt when no one came. I'd recently finished reading a book where one of the characters had said a prayer to "Our Lady of the Shooting Stars." I couldn't get that beautiful name out of my head. I had gone to Catholic school but never heard of her. I did some poking around and, apparently, she did not exist. She was born of the imagination of the author and had glued herself to mine. I picked up my guitar and started noodling some chord changes and pondering a mythic being named Our Lady of the Shooting Stars and thinking about my fear of failure and those steadfast, oceangoing birds.

The rest is hard to explain.

Somehow, a failed gig, a bout of crippling self-doubt

that shame-spiraled into existential fear of failure and a desperate desire for faith, plus several hundred soaring, screaming, hungry gulls crossing miles of open ocean without flapping their wings and a fictional, sacred name lifted out of a book led me to a song called "Our Lady of the Shooting Stars." Some sort of musical transubstantiation? Alchemy, for sure.

Non-narrative and non-linear, the song slowly grew into a metaphorical look at longing, awe, fear, hope, wonder, and a few other less nameable states of being. The "meaning" of this song, in a classic sense, is impossible to pin down. I hear different things in it every time I play it, and I'm not sure how I wrote it. The song is downright mysterious.

The first year I lived in Nashville, I was invited to a party at music photographer Jim McGuire's house that became a song circle with Guy Clark, Lyle Lovett, John Hiatt, Joe Ely, Steve Earle, and Nanci Griffith. It was a wonderful night, and I was on the edge of my seat, desperately wanting to go from being in the audience to swapping songs with that group of legends. I knew I was in deep waters, the new kid in town, but oh how I longed to sit in that circle. I'd deeply admired everyone in it for years.

As the music was winding down, Nanci looked over and asked, "Mary, would you play us a song?" I knew her because I'd opened a string of shows for her a month prior. I was absolutely thrilled when she invited me to play. I sat in the chair she offered, took her guitar into my hands, and played "Our Lady of the Shooting Stars."

The other songwriters closed their eyes and nodded as I played, some smiled. No wild applause, no pyrotechnics when the song ended. But the smiles and nods made me feel like I belonged. I still had a long way to go, but joining that circle was validation that moving to Nashville had been a good decision. Holding my own in that circle of songwriters whose records I owned and whose careers I followed gave me confidence. Being around songwriters I deeply admired humanized them and made the star I was reaching for feel less distant.

When I was done, I handed Nanci her guitar back. She shook her head and said, "Keep it." I froze, holding her engraved, signature sunburst Taylor 612 cutaway guitar in midair, question marks in both of my eyes.

"It's yours," she said. "When I moved to Nashville, Harlan Howard gave me his guitar. I'm giving you mine." I was speechless but somehow found the courage to say, "Will you sign it?" She signed, "For Mary, because YOU WILL sing."

I found out later it's an old Nashville tradition to pass on a guitar. It's an attempt to stay on the good side of the muse and the mystery. Some songwriters believe it is one way to keep songs flowing. Harlan gave Nanci one of his guitars because he felt there were no more songs left in it for him but there might be some in there for her. Nanci had done the same for me. Welcome to Nashville, kid. Remember to stay on the good side of mystery and paradox; they're your wheelhouse, now.

Who knows where songs come from? Could it really

have something to do with the guitar? Well, why not? Put seeds on a paper towel, add a little water, and in a couple days, watch what happens.

My friend, the late singer-songwriter Dave Carter, used to start off his live shows with, "Ladies and gentlemen, the stories I'll tell tonight are true. Of course, that doesn't mean they happened." The crowd would laugh, understanding what he meant. Dave's songs are mythic and dreamlike, two great places for mystery to take root.

In his song "Crocodile Man," Dave sings:

> *Mama she raised me on riddles and trances*
> *Fatback, channel-cat, lily white lies*
> *Rocked my cradle in a jimmy-crack fancy*
> *Never met papa and I never asked why*

Songs like "Crocodile Man" and "Our Lady of the Shooting Stars" are true to feeling, not fact. Imagination is where we go to discover new possibilities, what could be manifested, what is emotionally true. These songs take us below the surface of events to deeper places, accessing inner worlds facts cannot penetrate. There is much that is human that is not readily available in words, but we can point to a song and say, "This! This is how I feel." As a songwriter, there is an emotional honesty that I must adhere to, because while I don't have to have lived the things I sing about, I do have to believe them.

A song coming into the world is a living thing, a wild animal. My work is to not scare it away with too much scrutiny. Songs speed in and out along underground superhighways unmarked by road signs, a place where wild-eyed dogs jump out of ditches in front of headlights late at night. I try to quickly write down what I see, even if it's nonsense. Thinking at this point will scare the song away. This is not the time for analysis or editing.

So, when I get a quick glimpse of some wild-eyed ditch dog in my headlights, I hit the brakes, stop the car, get out, and follow her. If she runs into the woods, I run into the woods. If she suddenly turns around, looks at me, and becomes an angry parrot with a lit cigarette in one of her claws and the sound of my mother's voice coming out of her mouth, I nod and take note of what she is saying. My challenge is to keep going without knowing where I'm headed. I take disjointed images, hunches, thoughts, and feelings, combine them with ideas and visions, and mold these disparate clues into some kind of sequence. Dead-end roads abound, but if something feels right, I go with it.

Songs are a faint whisper from the future that pull from the past and seep into the present. A songwriter is the role of a medium, one eye in the now, one eye in memory, and a third eye focused on the other side of the thin veil of the future, trusting that it will somehow come together.

At some point, I'll get stuck. I have a verse and maybe a chorus, and it's starting to sound promising, and then, suddenly—nothing. Silence, crickets.

Getting stuck is part of the process. I'll have to decide,

do I abandon my half-written opus? If there is no taproot to some kind of deeper pull, I put it to the side. Not every song I start is mine to write. But if I feel that what I've started is connected to something compelling I can't yet see, I'll hang in and look for ways to keep it going.

A short nap is sometimes helpful. I'll lay down with a melody in my head and doze off. Sometimes I wake up with the right next word or idea as my first thought. The painter Salvador Dalí would doze in his chair in the afternoon with a glass in his hand, holding it over an empty pot. When he fell asleep, the glass would fall into the pot, make a clang, and wake him up. Then he'd paint his dream vision onto the canvas.

I also walk. I read in an interview somewhere that writers walk, and ever since then, I made walking a part of my writing practice. I'll head for the hills near my house in Nashville and climb until my heart pounds and sweat drips down the back of my neck. My melody will autoplay on repeat in the radio station in my head. I just listen. Walking can entice the song forward in some way; having my feet on the earth helps connect spirit to sky. On a few occasions, I have walked straight into an epiphany.

There is something sacred in the electricity that surges between song and songwriter. Lightning rod in hand, I follow flashes of ideas and inspiration. My work is to be a receiver. The process can be otherworldly, as if a visitor takes over my writing, then vanishes.

Sometimes I discover what a song "means" years after I've written it. Janis Ian said, "It's talent that leads. We're just trying to keep up. We usually throw things into songs that don't make a lot of sense at the time but feel right. Learning to listen to that small voice is what makes the difference."

Leonard Cohen said being a songwriter is much like being a Catholic nun; ultimately, we are married to a mystery. The best songs keep their inscrutability intact as they convey complex emotion across borders and boundaries.

Six

MERCY NOW: ACCESSING THE UNIVERSAL

Mercy Now

My father could use a little mercy now
The fruits of his labor
Fall and rot slowly on the ground
His work is almost over
Won't be long, he won't be around
I love my father, and he could use some mercy now

My brother could use a little mercy now
He's a stranger to freedom
Shackled to his fears and doubt
The pain that he lives in is
Almost more than living will allow
I love my brother, and he could use some mercy now

My Church and my Country could use a little mercy now
As they sink into a poisoned pit
That's going to take forever to climb out
They carry the weight of the faithful who follow them down
I love my Church and Country and they could use some
    mercy now

Every living thing could use a little mercy now
Only the hand of grace can end the race
Towards another mushroom cloud
People in power, well

They'll do anything to keep their crown
I love life, and life itself could use some mercy now

Yea, we all could use a little mercy now
I know we don't deserve it
But we need it anyhow
We hang in the balance
Dangle 'tween hell and hallowed ground
Every single one of us could use some mercy now
Every single one of us could use some mercy now

—Mary Gauthier

I was sitting on my bed in a small motel room in Canada thinking about my father. He'd wrecked his car on the way to Rouses grocery in Thibodaux and landed upside down in a ditch. Taken by ambulance to the hospital, he ended up in withdrawal from alcohol, suffering TIAs, small strokes of the brain that left him with Alzheimer's-like symptoms. He was moved into a home with an around-the-clock nurse.

My sister called to tell me he was not improving, and I should go see him while I still could. So I got on a plane. I stopped along the way from the airport to pick him up a couple packs of Fruit of the Loom T-shirts, some boxer shorts, a half dozen pairs of new socks, things my sister said he needed.

When I arrived a nurse was sitting in a chair guarding the only exit door. I asked her why she was blocking the door, and she said my father had walked out into the street and almost got hit by a car. He became agitated when she stopped him from going outside again. She looked exhausted. I thanked her for watching over him. She said he was in his bedroom. I approached hesitantly, poked my head in, "Hey, Daddy, how are you?"

He looked up from the bed where he was sitting, fully

clothed, shoes on, staring at the wall. "We have to stop them."

I said, "Daddy, it's Mary, do you know who I am?"

"We have to go, now!! LET'S GO! Stop them!!"

I put my hand on his shoulder, "Daddy, why don't you lay down? Can I lay down next to you? Let's rest?"

He ignored me, got up, walked to the kitchen, and started pacing. The nurse flinched, thinking he was going to try to bolt again. He started searching drawers and cabinets, and I asked him what he was looking for. He said he needed to write something down, NOW. I found a yellow legal pad and a pencil and handed them to him. Then my father, a man known for beautiful penmanship since he was a boy, sat perfectly straight at the kitchen table and proceeded to write gibberish, scratches that looked like the scrawled lines of a preschooler. He held the legal pad up to his chest, looked up, and said, "Sir, no, sir. I cannot answer that question, sir."

Was he on the witness stand in some kind of military tribunal in his mind? Was he back in Korea, where he'd served two years in counterintelligence during the Korean War? He'd never spoken of the war or his service. I had no reference for what he was saying.

His face had taken on a smooth, healthy glow. His skin was clearer than I'd ever seen it. Before the wreck he was a daily drinker and three-pack-a-day smoker. Had he forgotten he smoked and drank? The thousands of broken capillaries in his face that had covered him from ear to ear, caused by decades of alcoholism, were healing. He looked twenty years younger than the last time I saw him, but his mind was gone. He lost what he was saying in mid-sentence, got confused, put the pencil and paper down, and went back to his bedroom and sat on the bed and began staring again. I followed behind him.

He said, "Where's my rosary? Can we pray the rosary?"

His rosary was on the nightstand next to his bed. I picked it up and handed it to him. As he reached for it, I saw veins and bones sticking up from under the thin skin on his hands and arms, along with clusters of dark brown age spots and IV bruises and scars.

I winced and reached for his hand and held it against my heart. I hadn't held my father's hand in over forty years.

He looked at me for a moment.

Then, he said, "Baby, Daddy is dying."

His voice had the sweetest tone. Gentle, kind. No alcoholism, no paranoia, no dark angels. No cruelty. He spoke in the most peaceful, loving way.

I did not know this man, or who he thought he was. I no longer knew myself, either. Our roles had reversed. I was the parent, he the child. I felt the urge to protect him, keep him safe from harm. Our war was over, the fight no longer fair. The thought of ever battling him, mortifying.

I suddenly loved my father in a new way, a love void of expectations. I loved him dearly, beyond my understanding of love. I pushed down tears and prayed a silent prayer for Joe Gauthier. I prayed for mercy, for his suffering to stop. Then I put my arms around my father and held him close.

I drove back to the New Orleans airport, dropped off the rental car, and flew to Canada, arriving in Canso, Nova Scotia, two days before I was scheduled to play the Stan

Rogers Folk Festival. With plenty of time, I checked into my little room at the Last Port Motel and pulled out my guitar. As I played, I thought of my father as a young boy, tried to picture him as a child, the boy who never met his own father, whose single mother worked all the time at her little restaurant, Jenny's Café. I thought about what it must have been like for him to be raised by his grandmother, a woman who spoke only Italian and went to church twice a day in a black dress, black shoes, a black lace veil over her face. I'd spent my whole life fighting my father. But now, I hurt for him. His life would soon be coming to an end, and what I most wanted for him was mercy.

I picked a simple G/C/D pattern on the guitar, hitting alternate base notes with my thumb. Mumbled nonsense words, ended the lines with "my father, Mercy, Mercy Mercy . . . now."

Then I thought of my brother, his struggles with the criminal justice system, his rage. On hotel stationery, I wrote:

My brother and my father
Sure could use a little mercy from you now
They're both sunk into a darkness so dark
They can't find their way out
The hurt that they live in
Is almost more than living will allow
My brother and my father Lord
Sure could use a little mercy now from you

Jesus said the kingdom of heaven
Is here and now

So forget about the by and by
And do a little work around the house
Well my daddy and my brother Lord
What is that all about?
Yea my brother and my father
Sure could use a little mercy from you now

I played the little chord progression to these words for about an hour, humming the first melody that came. I dropped the kingdom of heaven stuff, the house cleaning stuff. Too preachy. Too surface level.

I rewrote it:

My brother and my father
Could use a little Mercy from you now
They're lost in a darkness
So black, they can't find their way out
The hurt that they carry
Is almost more than living will allow
My brother and my father,
Lord, they could use Mercy from you now.

I thought about my mother and my sister, maybe they should be here as well?

I wrote:

My sister and my mother
Could use a little mercy now
They're anchored in a hurt
That keeps dragging them down

Their hearts are beating heavy
There are things a heavy heart can't live without
My sister and my mother
Could use a little Mercy now

I played those two verses for hours. Nothing new came, so I went to lunch at the little motel café. At lunch it hit me that the Lucinda Williams song "Changed the Locks" had the same general form as this mercy song I was working on, so I pulled it up on my laptop, and sure enough, "Changed the Locks" repeats the first line of each verse as the last line, an old blues form. I stared at it and noticed the camera lens on Lu's song backed up after a few verses. She went from "changing the locks" on her front door in the beginning to "changed the tracks" under the train.

VI
I changed the lock on my front door so you can't see me any-more

VIIII
I changed the tracks underneath the train so you can't find me again

That was a very cool move. Maybe I should back the camera up in my song, move the narrator's perspective from family to the wider lens of the larger world? Zoom out?

It was July 2003, and the post-9/11 outpouring of love and goodwill for America had been erased by the March 2003 U.S. invasion of Iraq. As I traveled the world, I saw anti-American sentiment rising everywhere. I had an American flag guitar soft carrying case, and the glares I received carrying it on my back through international airports during this time told me all I needed to know.

I thought of all the lives on both sides soon to be ruined and lost by this war, and it made my heart ache. I opposed the invasion of Iraq with everything inside me, but to no avail.

At the same time, the *Boston Globe* was uncovering widespread and systemic child sex abuse in the Catholic Church, revealing a horrifying number of pedophile priests in the Boston area. Catholic priests from my old neighborhood were on TV in clerical collars and handcuffs. I thought of my Catholic parents and grandparents, of all the true believers, how they'd been betrayed. That's when the next lines started coming:

> *My church and my country*
> *Could use a little Mercy now*
> *They're mired in a sink hole*
> *It's gonna take forever to climb out*
> *They carry the weight of the faithful who follow them down*
> *I love my church and country*
> *They could use some Mercy now*

The scenes were expanding from my own deeply personal story to the bigger world around me. I didn't want the song to get stuck in a specific political moment, so I intentionally made the language poetic, metaphorical, like Lu did with "Changed the Locks."

Adding to my fear and foreboding, North Korea was conducting nuclear weapons tests, and the media was reporting on the likelihood of rogue states and terrorist groups obtaining enriched uranium. The proliferation of nuclear weapons was a threat to every living thing.

I wrote,

> *The nations of the earth*
> *Could use a little mercy now*
> *The atom bomb keeps changing hands*
> *And there's no telling when where or how*
> *The people of this planet*
> *Are chained beneath a giant mushroom cloud*
> *The nations of this earth*
> *Could use some mercy now*

Now I needed to tie everything together, bring it home. I thought for a while, and what came to me was a recent conversation I'd had with Bobby, my recovery sponsor, after a record label passed on me, a record deal I thought for sure I'd landed. I told Bobby I felt I deserved more than just a casual rebuff after having been courted for months.

Bobby laughed, then he said with a smile in his voice, "Given some of the behaviors you've exhibited in your life, you should thank God each and every day for NOT getting what you truly deserve." He suggested I pray, hat in hand, and say, "Lord, thank you for not giving me what I truly deserve." Bobby taught me that grace is getting what you don't deserve, and mercy is not getting what you do deserve.

I needed to be taught humility. How to be right sized. It occurred to me that maybe institutions like nations and religions might need the same thing? Maybe they too should pray that they never get what they truly deserved? I thought of Hiroshima and Nagasaki. Wasn't there a karmic price to be paid for the deaths of those innocents? What did the United States of America truly deserve? Going from the deeply personal to the universal, then back to the deeply personal, felt right and true. As I considered this, the next verse became:

> Yea we all could use a little mercy now
> Even though we don't deserve it
> Looks like Mercy's the only honest game in town
> We hang in the balance,
> Dangle 'tween hell and hallowed ground
> And every single one of us
> Could use a little Mercy from you now.

Then I put the song down, let it marinate.

On Monday morning, I flew out of Halifax, Nova Scotia, to Canmore, British Columbia. I checked into another little motel, in the Canadian Rockies. I had several days off before I was to perform at the Canmore Folk Festival, so I went back to work on the song.

I saw right away the verse about my mother and sister did not belong. I removed it, and it opened the song up. My father and brother could now each have their own verse. As I began expanding and deepening their verses, the song came closer into view.

My father could use a little mercy now
The fruits of his labor
Fall and rot slowly on the ground
His work is almost over
It won't be long and he won't be around
I love my father, and he could use some mercy from you now

My brother could use a little mercy now
All he's ever known is His heart beats with fear and doubt
The prison pain that he lives in is
Almost more than living will allow
I love my brother, and he could use some mercy from you now

My Church and my Country could use a little mercy now
As they sink into a poisonous pit
It's going to gonna take forever to climb out
They carry the weight of the faithful who follow them down
I love my Church and Country they could use mercy now

The people of the earth
Every living thing could use a little mercy now
The bomb keeps changing hands
Fingers on the trigger
Politicians play with fire
They'll do anything to keep their crown
I love life, and life itself could use some mercy now

I guess Yea, we all could use a little mercy now
Even though I know we don't deserve it
Mercy's the only honest game in town

We hang in the balance
Dangle 'tween hell and hallowed ground
Every single one of us could use some mercy now
Every single one of us could use some mercy now

I worked on it for the next three days, changing one word at a time, meditating on the meaning, letting the new words sit a while, and it was slow going. I played it for a friend, a fellow songwriter, who encouraged me to be brave and play it on a side stage at a festival workshop we were going to share the next afternoon. So, I wrote the words on a piece of hotel room stationery. And in the afternoon on the last day of Canmore Folk Festival, August 2003, I taped those words onto the mic stand and played "Mercy Now" in front of an audience for the very first time.

I've played it on every stage at every show, every night, since.

I close my eyes when I sing. I tell myself I do it to focus on note placement, pitch, and the meaning of the words. I want to feel the lyric for real, not act. All true, but truer still: I close my eyes because I'm not comfortable looking at people when I sing. When asked why he closed his eyes when he sang, Townes Van Zandt said, "Well, if the audience closed their eyes, I wouldn't have to."

Here's the reason: the human voice is the most unguarded of instruments, different from a trumpet, a piano, a guitar. Voice lives inside the body, in the throat, the lungs, deep inside the chest close to the heart. Maybe it's because

I'm not a trained vocalist, not a *singer*-singer, but singing makes me feel naked, exposed. Some say my singing is an acquired taste. One thing for sure, I've never had the ability to hold a note like some singers and bring an audience to their feet screaming, "Hell yeah!!" All this is to say: I know my voice suits my songs and conveys emotion. I sing convincingly, and for that I am grateful. But I have no sonic fig leaf to hide behind. My fear of looking people in the eye when I sing feels primal. I close my eyes to protect my heart.

Also, there are moments on stage, eyes closed, when I leave my body and fully enter the music. These moments are blissful. Time and space widen, deepen, then disappear. In those moments, I merge with the song. This liberation from self is akin to the narcotic high I fell in love with the first time I got high. But with dope, the need for more always kicked in, and there was never enough. With singing, the freedom from self is actual and is one of the great joys of performing. When my eyes are closed, I just let go and become one with the song. It lasts a few moments, a small, private escape that happens in public, and I re-enter my body satisfied. It's a feeling not unlike falling in love. Singing with my eyes closed feels right and good and sometimes even blissful.

I've never really questioned it, until the night I was invited to perform at the Nashville Rescue Mission in the summer of 2016. When I arrived, the auditorium was already overflowing. There was not a single empty seat, and men stood in the back and along the sides against the wall, waiting for the music. The overcrowded room grew warm. It smelled of unwashed bodies, dirty clothes, urine, and early-stage gangrene. Some men nodded out in the metal folding chairs, their heads resting on their chests. Others talked to themselves, mumbling.

Gospel singer Wayne Settles kicked it off with his big gospel voice and a full band. He soon had the men of all races, ages, and backgrounds smiling, clapping, and singing, some raising their hands up in the air. There were crutches, walkers, leg braces, back braces, and bandages; there were long gray beards and tattered, ill-fitting, dirty clothes; and, to my surprise, there were also younger men, well-kept, in clean clothes, who stared at the floor. They, too, slept at the mission.

When Wayne was done, a preacher took the podium and read from Corinthians. "Love is patient, love is kind. It does not envy, it does not boast, it is not proud. It does not dishonor others, it is not self-seeking, it is not easily angered, it keeps no record of wrongs."

Men responded, "Yes! Yes! Amen! Amen!"

I was invited to close the show solo, voice and guitar only, with a single song, "Mercy Now."

I knew I could not close my eyes. The men sitting in front of me had all been looked over, left behind. I could not be one more person who looked away. I had to meet their eyes as I sang.

I prayed for courage and sang, "My father could use a little mercy now." I looked directly into the face of a man in the front row. Our eyes met. He nodded gently. I nodded back. He smiled. I was not expecting the mutuality, but it turns out, I needed it.

I glanced at the man beside him. His face was disfig-ured. Grafted skin covered the area where his right eye once was. No matter. I looked directly into his misshapen face and sang, "the fruits of his labor fall and rot slowly on the ground." He returned my gaze, nodded yes, his one eye per-fectly capable of reciprocity.

I kept going. I looked into the eyes of the next fellow, and then the next. I'd get a yes, a grin, a green light. As I scanned the room, I realized there was nothing to fear here tonight. No need to protect my heart. These men and me, we needed the same things. Hope. Empathy. Acknowledg-ment. Respect.

Their nods, their grins, their faces said, "Sing, Mary, sing! Sing us the good news! Sing to us of mercy and forgive-ness. Show us your heart, that we might feel our own!"

They craved the mercy I sang of, desperately needed it. My eyes reflected back yes, me too, me too.

I was signing autographs after a show at the Edmonton Folk Festival in Alberta, when I saw a woman with a black lab service dog on a short leash standing in the back, wait-ing for the line to wind down. She approached the table when I was done and introduced herself. "Hi! My name is Carla!"

She paused, offered me a huge smile, glanced down at the lab. "And this is Lando." She spoke full mouthed, a lit-tle loud. Theater major, I thought.

She said, "I'm here to put in a request!"

Oh Lord, I thought. A request?

"I'm a music therapist at a hospice. I have a client who owned a record store downtown for years. He's a huge music fan, and a big fan of yours. He does not have long to live. It would mean a lot if you'd come sing for him before you leave."

She paused.

"I could come get you at your hotel tomorrow morning, bring you back. The whole thing would probably take about an hour."

Oh boy. What to say?

I'd not been inside a hospice since AIDS had taken the lives of so many of my close friends twenty years prior. Returning to hospice was scary. It could conjure ghosts.

I needed a minute. I looked down. Tried to think.

The process of dying is an intimate, intensely personal unfolding. In addition to worrying about stirring up grief from my past, I was afraid of invading a private moment, maybe even adding to a family's distress. How could I go into a hospice room with a frightened family I'd never met, open up my guitar case, pull out my guitar, and start singing?

"Carla, this scares me."

She smiled, grabbed my arm, lowered her voice. "Mary, I'll walk you through it. Lando and I do this every day. Just follow our lead."

I hesitated. I really didn't want to do it.

"It would mean a lot to Robert," she said.

I'd met men like Robert over the years, music lovers and

true friends to singer-songwriters like me. Robert probably sold my records one at a time, suggesting each person give my music a listen. I felt indebted, torn.

I looked at Lando, his shiny black coat, sweet face, beautiful eyes.

I caved.

"Ok. All right."

The next morning I stood nervously sipping hot coffee by the valet station at 9:45 a.m., wishing I'd said no. I was not looking forward to going to a hospice to sing for a dying man.

Carla pulled up in a van, head bobbing, singing along with the radio. She waved, smiled, hit a button, the side door of the van slid open, and the music got louder. I tossed in my guitar.

Lando surrendered the passenger seat to me, hopped in the back, and poked his face through the space between the two front seats. I petted his head and tried not to think about where we were going. We drove through downtown Edmonton, making small talk, until we arrived at the hospice. As we headed in Lando stayed by Carla's side, no leash.

At the nurses' station, the nurses smiled, petted Lando. Carla introduced me. I explained that I was a songwriter, lived in Nashville, was in town for the weekend. As we made our way down the hall, Carla said she'd spoken to Robert's wife and she was expecting us.

The door was cracked open, the room dark. Carla gave a little knock, announced herself, marched in, and turned on the overhead fluorescents. The room lit up, brightly. Lando stayed by her side, ears up, tail wagging. I followed a few steps behind them, hesitant, my guitar in a soft case on my shoulder.

Robert was unconscious. His wife sat in a chair by the side of his bed. Carla gave her a quick hug. Robert had been unconscious for forty-eight hours. His breathing, shallow. The doctors weren't sure he'd regain consciousness. His wife had dark circles under her eyes.

Carla patted Robert's bed two times, and Lando jumped up on it. He lay down next to Robert and rested his head on Robert's chest. He gazed at Robert's unconscious face. Carla bent down over Robert and shouted, "Mary Gauthier is here! She's here to sing for you! Isn't that wonderful!"

No response.

Carla shouted again, her face lowered directly next to Robert's left ear, "ROBERT WAKE UP! MARY GAUTHIER IS HERE TO SING FOR YOU!"

She put a hand on his shoulder, and her other hand grabbed his hand and held it. He did not respond.

Carla nodded at me. Your turn.

Sing. Now.

I pulled my guitar out of the case, tuned it, put on my harmonica holder, and nervously started "Mercy Now." I focused on the meaning of every word. After the last note rang out, I was hoping for a miracle, but Robert's eyes remained closed. He had not moved. The room was silent. We all watched, waited.

Then, his lips slightly moved. His wife jumped up from

her chair. Carla shouted directly into his ear, "Robert, WHAT DID YOU SAY?"

Robert's lips moved ever so slightly, and a faint, frail sound came out. Carla, trying to make out what he was saying, her ear almost on his lips, broke out into a smile.

She turned to us and said, "Robert says he is richly blessed."

A lump formed in my throat. My worries about conjuring ghosts or being invasive suddenly seemed selfish, petty. This was about Robert and the song, not me. I put my guitar down, reached for Robert's hand and squeezed it. He squeezed back, softly. Strangers no more.

I'd done nearly nothing, and now a dying man felt richly blessed? And his wife would have a few more hours with him awake, before he passed? All because of a song?

A song!

I remember an interview with the brilliant Canadian songwriter Ferron. When asked about her transcendent song "Testimony" she said, "What is the formula for writing a song like that? I don't know, to almost die? Be very depressed and not know who you are or who your father is or where you're going or what the purpose of life is and why does everybody hate each other and why did they hurt me? If you put all that together and sit down somewhere and weep, you might write 'Testimony.' It's not a craft. Survival was the craft."

How could writing this incredible song be in service to

the songwriter's urgent need to survive the traumas she carried? It was done by connecting the deeply personal to the whole.

Ferron wrote:

They say slowly
Brings the least shock
But no matter how slow I walk
There are traces
Empty spaces
And doors and doors of locks
But by my life be I spirit
And by my heart be I woman
And by my eyes be I open
And by my hands be I whole

This song is about her, yes, but it is also about me. It's about all of us. The deeply personal is what connects each of us to the universal. The severing of that connection (through trauma, addiction, etc.) is life-threatening, the re-joining, a fundamental component of survival.

"Mercy Now" came to me as a prayer in a time when loved ones and the world around me were sinking into darkness. The song brought catharsis, and then, unexpectedly, it brought something else. The desperation I'd felt, laced with anger and fear, began to give way to a new calm. I began to feel connected.

A decade after I wrote it, *Rolling Stone* called "Mercy Now" one of the "Top 20 saddest songs of all time." I'm honored to have one of my songs in a *Rolling Stone* top-twenty-of-all-time poll, but "Mercy Now" is not sad, it's real. People sometimes cry when they hear it, but if tears come, I think they are tears of resonance; the words provide listeners a witness to their struggle. "Mercy Now" started as a personal song, then it deepened. It became universal.

Every summer, I teach songwriting at folk festivals around the United States and the United Kingdom. I work with songwriting students in fairly large groups, and I've noticed that often a student's first song draft is what I call a "polite cocktail party" version of a thorny, emotionally difficult story. The idea for the song is there, but it's hiding underneath politeness. The song bounces along the surface so as to not upset anyone, including the songwriter. The songwriter is writing *about* the story rather than writing the story. The song feels removed because it is removed. There is a deeper story there, underneath the niceties, superficialities, and distance.

My job, then, is to help guide the students back to the original inspiration for their song. I ask the writers to tell me the story behind it, the one they'd tell their best friend late at night over a bottle of wine by candlelight. That story always contains conflict. What they are hiding in their polite versions is the real song asking to be born.

The safe, innocuous surface story in the first draft is just the beginning. The deeper song, their emotional truth, needs to be encouraged, the writers reassured that their

story, their real story, matters. Beyond hiding, diary reading, and navel gazing, at the core of every human being
lives the soul, that tender place that holds secrets that we
protect and defend. This is where the universal resides,
way down, in the deeply personal. And the more specific
you get, the more universal the song becomes. The deeply
personal IS universal. And it is the universal that makes for a
good song. As the poet Rainer Maria Rilke said, "Our deepest fears are like dragons guarding our deepest treasures."
Those deepest treasures are unborn songs waiting to be
written.

Songs ask this of the songwriter: Be vulnerable. Be
brave. Be true. There is a benevolent force trying to push
the truth to the surface so that the writer (and the world)
can see it. When songwriters are willing to bravely reveal
the deeper truths cowering behind walls of self-protection,
their songs begin to resonate. Songs are where we can
safely tell secrets. A form of self-expression, yes, but even
more importantly, a form of emotional communication.

I try to point songwriting students down the road to
their own voice, which is often the voice they are most terrified of. When they land on the sound of their own voice
by revealing the deeper truth of their song, they often
weep. The voice that makes them weep is theirs and theirs
alone, but it is also bigger than the individual and connected to the universal, the whole. That voice is mighty. It
is as important as any voice ever raised. Once a writer finds
their own voice, they can't forget that it exists. I hope my
students will go out into the world and use that voice. It's
their decision, but if I do my job, they are now aware that

they are making a decision to use, or not use, their own voice. This is what I do my best to teach.

My father did not live long enough for me to play "Mercy Now" for him, but I always think of him when I play it, and it helps me feel connected to him, still.

Seven

GOODBYE:
SONGS AS SEERS

Goodbye

Born a bastard child in New Orleans
To a woman I've never seen
Don't know if she ever held me
All I know is she let go of me

So I passed through like thunder
I passed through like rain
Passed out from under
Goodbye could have been my family name.

Every time I settle down it happens
I get a restless feeling I can't control
I hit the wall then I hit the highway
I've got the curse of a gypsy on my soul

So I move through like thunder
I move through like rain
Moving out from under
Goodbye could have been my family name.

I can't break free of the winds that blow me
They roll in like a Gulf Coast Hurricane
I'd like to stay now but I don't know how
Hold me honey till I'm gone again

When it's time to leave forever
I pray the Lord don't take me slow
I don't know where I'm going
Just let me say goodbye and go

And I'll push though like thunder
I'll push through like rain
Pushed out from under
Goodbye could have been my family name
Goodbye could have been my family name
Goodbye could have been my family name

—Mary Gauthier

I was born in March '62 and adopted from St. Vincent's that November by Barbara and Joe Gauthier, a young Catholic couple from Thibodaux, Louisiana. Family legend had it they'd waited years for Catholic Charities to approve their adoption request. When they got the green light to pick up their baby, I was already almost a year old because I had had an umbilical hernia pushing on the muscles of my abdominal wall around my navel, and the orphanage did not want to release me until it had healed. Imperfections notwithstanding, I was their first child. Four and a half years later, they returned to the same orphanage and adopted a son who would become my brother Michael, then my mother got pregnant and gave birth to my sister, Michelle. To me, these were unemotional facts, and for the first four decades of my life, I never gave them a second thought.

The one romance I still have with my origin story is that I am proud to have been born in New Orleans, the old city parish on the Mississippi River. A haunted beauty of a town, there is nowhere else on earth like it. Part Native American, part French, part Spanish, part African, part antebellum American South, she is known by many names. The Big Easy, the City That Care Forgot, Nola, the Crescent City. New Orleans is a gumbo of incredibly complex race relations, the birthplace of jazz, zydeco, swamp pop, and brass hop, and host to a massive treasure chest of other musical riches, some of the best food in the world, painters, poets, playwrights, authors, alcoholics, dysfunction, and debauchery, all mixed together in the thick, swampy heat.

The first time I performed in New Orleans was as part of a Louisiana Music concert series at the Ogden Museum of Southern Art. I introduced my song "Goodbye" by telling the audience my unmarried mother gave birth to me at St. Vincent de Paul's in New Orleans, and I was adopted through Catholic Charities when I was about a year old. I did it to assert my New Orleans bona fides and let the audience know I qualified as a Louisiana artist even though I now lived in Nashville. It was the first and only time I ever said those things on stage.

After the show, a woman came to the table where I was signing CDs and told me her mother was a volunteer at St. Vincent's, one of many women in a Catholic baby-holding group.

She said, "In the early '60s nuns at St. Vincent's were overwhelmed by the large number of children in the facility. Newborns and infants were going un-held for days, if not weeks. Catholic women throughout the city were recruited to help cuddle, feed, and diaper. My mom volunteered for years."

Overcrowded? Too many babies? This was the first I'd heard about this. Whoa . . . was it possible that this woman's mother had held me? I forced a smile, thanked her, and asked her to please thank her kind mother for me. She promised she would.

"I've always relied on the kindness of strangers," I used to say with a smile in a whispery female voice. It was my intentionally bad imitation of Blanche DuBois from the Tennessee Williams play *A Streetcar Named Desire*, my attempt at dark humor: lesbian tomboy me as the tragic femme fatale who lived in a state of perpetual panic about fading beauty, unable to separate fantasy from reality, constantly mistaking dependency and kindness as one and the same. As an adoptee from New Orleans, the line resonated, and I enjoyed making a dark joke out of it, especially with other adoptees. I thought it was funny but had no idea how true the "joke" might have been.

As she was writing my check, Libra LaGrone, the director of the Ogden Museum Louisiana Music series, offered to take me to lunch at Casamento's Restaurant. I gladly accepted.

The next day as we were driving down Magazine Street, she surprised me by saying, "You know, Mary, St. Vincent's is right up there on the right. It's a rooming house now. Do you want to see it?" She hit the brakes, pulled over, and parked.

I had no time to answer.

St. Vincent's? It had somehow never entered my mind that the orphanage where I was born was an actual place or that it still existed. Why was I breaking out in a cold sweat as I looked out the passenger window at St. Vincent's for the first time?

Clearly once a proud and mighty New Orleans Catholic institution, St. Vincent's had decayed into a slum. At first glance, I saw rickety fire escapes, dilapidated, sagging wooden porches, and rusted Spanish ironwork running the length of rotting balconies.

"Want to go in?" Libra asked.

I nodded, caught up in the moment, "Why not?"

We got out of the car and walked toward the entrance past an unshaven man in rumpled, dirty clothes with an unlit cigarette hanging from the side of his mouth. He was cursing under his breath, carrying two old suitcases, and kicking a cardboard box of clothes in the direction of a beat-up old truck. There was a small group of men sitting on the front porch stairs, drinking from brown paper bags, smoking. I nodded hello. They nodded back.

St. Vincent's Guest House seemed to be a cut-rate demi-monde, a crash pad for down and outs, addicts, drunks, prostitutes, johns. The Catholics made their exit decades ago. Bums, transients, and boozy lost souls entered, looking for some fabled New Orleans good times, a little *laissez les bons temps rouler* on the cheap. As I climbed the stairs, I saw chiseled into a white marble stone embedded in the wall of the building to the right of the large wooden front door:

St. Vincent De Paul's Woman's and Infant Asylum

I read it again.

Infant Asylum.

My God. This was the door my birth mother walked through pregnant with me in '61. The door she walked out of, without me, in '62. It was the door my new parents walked through to get me, and the door they walked out of with an eleven-month-old baby in their arms.

Me.

Asylum.

I was in shock. I knew I didn't have to go in. But I also knew I was going in. There was no turning back. As soon as I made the decision to keep going, I felt the comforting sensation of benevolent forces protecting and guiding me.

Guardian angels.

When I was a child my mother came to my bedroom at night and tucked me in. We'd recite "Angel of God" together, a plea for the intercession of guardian angels, a common prayer taught to young Catholic children.

> Angel of God,
> my guardian dear
> To whom God's love had put me here
> Ever this day be at my side
> To light and guard to rule and guide.
> Amen

The prayer resonated. It's the one thing I still embrace from my Catholic upbringing. In head-on collisions with life-altering events, I know I'm not alone. I felt guardian angels with me as I entered St. Vincent's.

Libra walked behind me.

The lobby floor was made of Italian marble, old and cracked but still beautiful. There was a reception desk on the left with a disheveled man behind it. He wore thick glasses and a rumpled brown suit and continued looking down and shuffling papers as we walked up to him. An old-fashioned phone sat on the countertop; numbered room keys hung from a rack on the wall.

Before I could decide what to say, Libra blurted out, "Hello! How are you doing? Mary was adopted from here! Can we take a look around?"

The man looked up, expressionless. His indifference embarrassed me. Clearly, I was not the first former resident who'd walked through that terrifying front door. My heart ached for the other brave souls who'd made this pilgrimage only to find a disinterested desk clerk in a run-down rooming house. He grunted, and we walked past him through the foyer out into the courtyard.

A disintegrating statue of the Virgin Mary stood in tall uncut grass next to a crumbling Stations of the Cross. Across the courtyard, there was a dirty fenced-in swimming pool and, beyond that, a closed-off boarded-up building. Institutional looking, medical. Was that the maternity hospital where babies were born? Where I was born?

Jesus.

The formality of the structure chilled me. Like courthouses I'd been in, it was the architecture of intimidation, built to clarify who has power and who does not. This "home" for unwed mothers must have served to keep my unmarried pregnant mother in her place. Time, decay, neglect, and changing social mores had rendered this scene more creepy than scary, more pitiful than mighty. But back in '61 it must have been a terrifying place for an unmarried pregnant girl from a small Louisiana town to find herself.

Up until this moment, my birth mother existed only in some distant and misty realm, as a phantom, more an idea than a reality.

Standing in the courtyard of this rotting institution, my mind blew open. Mysterious strangers connected by blood, far-off ghosts started to stir. My birth mother became real to me, a vulnerable, terrified girl with few choices, pregnant, unmarried, hiding in this institution with other girls like her, their agency taken away by shame, lack of money, and oppressive cultural standards they'd failed to live up to. I had known my own pain for a long time, but that day I began to feel hers too. In that moment, instead of simply feeling for myself, I began to feel the suffering of another screwed-up young woman: my birth mother.

Libra and I went back inside.

We walked down a long hallway; paint was peeling off the ceiling in thick sheets, and the moldy carpet was coming up in lumps. We stopped at the bottom of a wooden stairway to stare at a large framed black-and-white photo. It was a picture of the St. Vincent orphans, circa late fifties / early sixties, children arranged by height on a stairway; infants in bassinets lined the floor at the bottom of the steps. A little boy sat on a tiny wooden rocking horse next to a nun, who stood sternly to the side wearing a starched white headpiece the size of a tablecloth.

Babies in baskets and toddlers in donated clothes gazed into the camera with one god-awful thing in common: a dazed, wide-eyed, empty stare. Even the newborns stared with the vacant look of prisoners of war, the deadened look of people in a concentration camp. I scanned the photo carefully, looking for myself. I have no infant photos, so even if I was there, I probably couldn't find myself. Not being able to identify myself in the picture didn't mean I wasn't there.

A flash of anger shot through me. Would these children, now adults, want to be on display like this in the lobby of this most unholy place? For a moment, I considered pulling the photograph off the wall and running down Magazine Street with it, but the thought was fleeting. I could not save them now. But maybe, I could save myself.

Therapists had suggested adoption shaped me, but I never bought their theories. They seemed distant, taken from a textbook written by an academic white-haired white man. I argued that I didn't remember anything before the age of three, and besides, babies do not retain early memories, right? What I could not remember could not hurt me, I said, but something did hurt. And it had hurt for a long, long time.

"I'm done," I told Libra. "Let's go. Enough of this sadness-and-loss-a-thon. Let's go get an oyster po-boy!"

We went to Casamento's and dropped the subject of orphans, adoption, and St. Vincent's. We made small talk over po-boys, then Libra brought me back to my hotel.

I couldn't get the picture of the babies out of my mind. Finally, I picked up the phone and called my adoptive mother and asked her what I was like when she and my father picked me up from St. Vincent de Paul's.

"Mary," she told me. "When we got you, there was

something wrong with you. You didn't laugh, you didn't cry, you didn't look left or right. You didn't blink. You just stared straight ahead. You didn't respond to anything or anyone. I remember saying to your father, 'Joe, there's something wrong with this baby.' But after a few weeks of me playing with you and holding you, you began to snap out of it."

It was the first time I'd heard this story.

My story.

I was in my forties now. I'd begun working with my first therapist several years earlier, after yet another one of my romantic relationships had fallen apart spectacularly. One day, the therapist showed up to our session with a pink baby blanket. She handed it to me and said, "Mary, you were not received with loving arms on the day you were born. I want to gift you with this receiving blanket."

Receiving blanket? I never heard of such.

She said the blanket was symbolic; to officially welcome me into the world and encourage me to welcome myself. She strongly suggested I find my birth mother and learn my story. She hinted that I would remain stuck in addictive, dead-end relationships until I did. I didn't believe her.

I took the pink blanket from her, touched the soft cotton. I smiled. Pink was the wrong color. Blue would be wrong too. I figured I was more or less a purple receiving blanket kind of person (if I were to ever be received by a blanket), but this adult baby blanket crap was not for me. I did not seriously consider looking for my birth mother. I figured when she gave me away, she meant it. It was a done deal. My mother's name is Barbara Gauthier. End of story.

But it was not the end of the story. A new journey was beginning for me, even though I didn't know it, yet. I was a grown-ass woman, not looking for another mommy, but I sure was looking for peace.

After months of wavering, I finally decided to make a small step in the direction of a secret search. I called Catholic Charities and asked if they could send me my files. The woman on the phone said she'd send what she had on my case. I thought, well, that was easy. This isn't so bad.

A few weeks later, I received "Non-identifying information." I opened the letter in a fog. The document from Catholic Charities gave me a short history of my birth mother's family. It said she was twenty-one when she had me. She and my father were different religions. Because of their religions, they could not marry. One other thing the letter told me was that my birth mother named me Stacy, and the nuns named me Anastasia. I did not recognize either of these names.

My adoptive parents named me Mary because it was my mother's great-grandmother's name; she was my mother's father's mother, an Italian immigrant who'd died long before I was adopted. I was ambivalent about all three names.

The letter went on to say that because my mother had not inquired about me, her address could not be shared. There was nothing about my father.

My stomach sank. My heart hurt. I read the letter again. Then, I felt nothing. I went blank, like a turned-off TV. I put the Catholic Charities letter in a drawer, told no one about it, quit therapy, and shoved the entire process out of my mind for another five years. As the song said, "Goodbye" could have been my family name.

Ever since I could remember I'd wake up in the morning with dread pressing down on my stomach and chest— combined with a terrifying, untethered feeling of falling through space. I'd shower and shake it off, but the falling feeling left me anxious and afraid. I'd numbed it with booze and dope from the time I was thirteen years old, dealt with it as best I could. After I got sober, I went to a bazillion twelve-step meetings, therapy, the gym, and yoga studios; I hiked the woods, did energy healing, attended personal growth workshops, and read self-help books by the dozens, but the feeling remained. And my romantic relationships, one after the other, ended badly. Well, horribly.

I never made it much past two years with anyone, and the last year of every relationship found me terrified of abandonment, holding on to something no longer working. I jumped from relationship to relationship, never more than a few months between. Sobriety had only made this pattern more obvious. Before my visit to St. Vincent's, I wrote a song called "Goodbye." I thought it was a song about restlessness and the life of a troubadour:

> Born a bastard child in New Orleans
> To a woman I've never seen
> Don't know if she ever held me
> All I know is she let go of me
> So I passed through like thunder

I passed through like rain
Goodbye could have been my family name

Like other songs of its ilk, this song romanticized leaving. Leaving songs are almost all penned by men, the story always more or less the same. A woeful but adamant male narrator was called to roam, sorry to go but powerless to resist the pull of the highway. Absconsion was as inevitable as sunrise and sunset. But "Goodbye" was different. Truth be told, leaving was *not* something I wanted. Endlessly moving on from those I loved was not making me happy.

Ever since I picked up the guitar again sober, in the back of my mind, I had a hunch that someday I'd work on a project that I would call *The Foundling*. It was a vague notion, floating around since I'd first started writing songs, a hunch that persisted, year after year. I really didn't know what it meant.

Songwriting had opened a door I needed to walk through to begin to make sense of my life, but I did not know that yet. In retrospect, I think the idea of my album *The Foundling* was waiting for me to be ready for it. I had to live longer, see more, and visit St. Vincent's first. There was so much inside me I did not understand, so many blind spots.

Turns out, my songs were always ahead of me. I was always trying to catch up with a mysterious strange knowing. Each new song was an opportunity to go beyond where I'd been. My work was to pull each song into existence little by slow, and the song somehow then pulled *me* more into existence. The experience is like wandering inside a dark cave with a box of matches. Light a match, quickly take in the surroundings, write what you see, the match burns out. Blackness returns. Strike another match. Repeat.

I did not know what I was looking for or what I would find. I was wandering a dark, unlit cavern. *The Foundling* would be an exploration of this deep, dark cave I had no name for. It would be a collection of songs about a baby left at St. Vincent's.

The Foundling was me.

Eight

BLOOD IS BLOOD: AWAKENING

Blood Is Blood

Clouds are spreading like bruises on the evening sky
I walk the streets alone again tonight
It starts to rain still I search each passing face
Blood is blood and blood don't wash away
Blood is blood and blood don't wash away

When I was a child, they told me she loved me too much
She didn't keep me 'cause my mama loved me too much
She left without a trail she left without a trace
But blood is blood and blood don't wash away
Blood is blood and blood don't wash away

I got a heart that's ripped I got a soul that's torn
I got a hole in me like I was never born

Blood is thicker than water blood is bound by God
I don't know who I am I don't know who I'm not
I don't know my name I can't find my place
Blood is blood and blood don't wash away
Blood is blood and blood don't wash away
Blood is blood and blood don't wash away
Blood is blood and blood don't wash away

I walk the streets alone again tonight

—Mary Gauthier and Crit Harmon

Walking the grounds of St. Vincent's shook the whisper of *The Foundling* from the back of my mind to the front and made it fully conscious and urgent. I was suddenly on a mission. For a few days, I seriously considered renting a room at St. Vincent's Guest House to begin the writing process. A trusted friend looked at me like I'd lost my mind when I mentioned it. So instead of heading back to New Orleans, I went into research mode.

I bought every book I could find on the subject of adoption. I devoured dozens, searching for inspiration, information, and song ideas. Most of the books did not speak to me, but I found a couple that did. The first was Nancy Verrier's *The Primal Wound: Understanding the Adopted Child*. Verrier is a therapist and the mother of an adopted daughter. She repeatedly used the words "adoption" and "trauma" together, and for the first time, I had a sense of what *The Foundling* song cycle would be about: Adoption trauma.

Was this really *me*? If this was true, and I was still not sure it was, what else about myself didn't I know? Should I treat my early childhood as a cold case? Maybe childhood trauma IS a cold case?

I found another writer on adoption whose work deeply spoke to me: Betty Jean Lifton, an adoptee and

adoption-reform advocate whose books are searing con-
demnations of the secrecy that traditionally shrouded closed
adoption. In her memoir *Twice Born* she wrote: "Society, by
sealing birth records, by cutting adoptees off from their
biological past, by keeping secrets from them, has made
them into a separate breed, unreal even to themselves."

Well, yeah.

Me.

There was so much I did not yet know, so much still to
learn. I'd spent most of my life believing I should first and
foremost be grateful for being adopted. I believed asking
questions about my origins would create a problem, so I
never asked. I pledged allegiance and kept questions about
my birth mother in a vault deep in the back of my mind. I
did not allow myself to open it. Or even approach it.

Until I started my research for *The Foundling*, it had not
occurred to me that other adoptees also felt this urgency
around gratitude. I don't think my adoptive parents forced
their need for it on me, but for decades, it felt important to
not ask questions.

This was all about to change.

It took forty-odd years for me to get here, but I was
awakening from a deep sleep. A bewildering journey of
the soul had me wondering about the truth about my life,
no matter how difficult it might be to swallow.

My birth certificate says I was born on March 11, 1962.
The letter I'd gotten from Catholic Charities said I was
born on March 3, 1962. I don't know which date is correct.
I probably never will. Upon my adoption, the state of Louisiana sealed my original birth certificate, with my birth

parents' names on it, in perpetuity. A new document with my adoptive parents' names on it was created. My second birth certificate, a legal document, is the only birth certificate I have ever been allowed to see. I began to understand that in a closed adoption system, adoptees are cut off from our heritage by the power of the state and expected to believe that our life began on the day we were adopted, the exact story I'd internalized my entire life.

I continued reading and found another powerful book on adoption, *Wanderers All* by Gregory Armstrong. It is the story of generational trauma; Armstrong's parents were both adopted, and he offers deep insights into how the past affects our present lives, even when we are unaware of it.

"I have no close friends. I'm what's called a loner, the silent one off in the corner. After all these years I'm still walking the streets of New York alone at night. Walking in circles, headed nowhere."

I knew that feeling.

I called my old friend and producer/co-writer Crit Harmon and asked him if he would help me, and together we began working Gregory's imagery into "Blood Is Blood," the first song for *The Foundling* song cycle.

Writing this song gave me permission to ask questions I'd never dared ask. How was I supposed to make sense of what I was told as a child, that my mother loved me so much she gave me away?

I couldn't.

I called Catholic Charities back. I found the woman I'd spoken to years before and asked her if there was any way she might help me find my birth mother, my story. "Please," I begged.

She said "Sweetie, I don't know what to tell you. The law is the law. I cannot unseal files. But I do have an idea. There is a woman I know named Lee Ann who has helped other people in their search. She's not in the search business anymore, but maybe she can guide you. I'll give you her name and number. You give her a call." I thanked her, wrote down Lee Ann's information, and hung up. I stared at Lee Ann's number for days. The songs were pushing me, asking me to be brave. They demanded this next thing of me, this thing I'd never imagined myself doing.

I called.

Lee Ann told me she, too, was an adoptee. She became interested in helping other adoptees after she reunited with her birth mother several years prior, but her birth mother had passed, and she was no longer doing searches.

I told her, "I'm not sure I even really want to find my birth mother, but I need to try. I am being pulled to it for reasons I do not fully understand."

There must have been something in my voice, because after a short silence, Lee Ann said she would help me. I told her I would send a deposit immediately. I figured the search would take months and likely end with no answers. She asked me the year and date on my birth certificate, asked me who I talked to at Catholic Charities.

A couple days later, I was driving through the Bronx on my way out of NYC after playing Joe's Pub, headed for my next show somewhere in Connecticut, when my mobile phone rang.

It was Lee Ann.

She said, "Hey, Mary, have you got a pen?"

"Yes, sure."

I pulled out a piece of paper from my book, a sheet of stationery from the Nyack Best Western, where I'd stayed when I played the Turning Point two nights prior.

Lee Ann said, "I found your mother. Her name is Yvette."

In one big blurt, she told me my mother's full name, her birth date, where she lived, her marital status, her maiden name, the value of her house, and her phone number.

I was writing as fast as I could, still driving. I didn't feel excited. I didn't feel happy. I didn't feel victorious. I didn't feel anything. It had not occurred to me that this information would be found. In three days? How did she do that? I looked at the Best Western stationery with the name and number of my birth mother on it and I wondered, who is this terrifying stranger? I knew I would never be able to call. I did not have the courage. But a plan was forming. I had to ask Lee Ann for one more thing.

"Lee Ann, would you call Yvette for me? Let her know I found her and want to talk to her? Tell her my name and number. Give her my website so she can see what I look like and what I do? I don't think I can do this without your help." I told her I'd pay her whatever she wanted.

Lee Ann agreed to make the call. I hung up and went back into denial. None of this was real. None of this was happening.

Two days later, Lee Ann called again. I was in the car driving somewhere in New York State. She said, "Mary, I just spoke to your mother."

"And?"

"She started crying when I told her who I was. She didn't deny that she was your mother. She didn't try to hang up. But she did seem startled and reluctant to give out any information."

Huh?

"She doesn't want to talk, yet. She said she needs time. I gave her your numbers, and I told her your website. She knows you want to talk to her, to meet her. She knows she's been found. She's aware of your interest in her."

"Why was she crying?"

"She seems like a sad woman, a woman who's had a hard life. She feels resigned, and of course she does! You have to understand when she signed you over to Catholic Charities, she gave up any right to ever see you again. She's had to accept that, and she has accepted it. She surrendered to it a long time ago. Give her time; she might come around. Let her think about this for a while."

"Ok. Yes, I will." I was both disappointed and relieved. I wanted to talk to my birth mother, but I was terrified to talk to her. I thanked Lee Ann, hung up, and began waiting.

Six months went by. I snapped back to my default perspective. None of this was happening. My birth mother was not real. Even Lee Ann was made of fairy dust.

Christmas was coming, and my girlfriend was pressuring me to call the number Lee Ann gave me. She argued that my birth mother must be afraid to call me. She said I should pick up the phone and call her because I said I wanted "a period at the end of this sentence." I was looking for her;

she was not looking for me. Set a hard deadline. Call her before Christmas.

I woke up one morning, a week before Christmas, and knew it was the day. It wasn't just that seven months had gone by since I had first gotten Yvette's name and number, it was that I was stuck: I had not been able to write another good song for *The Foundling* song cycle. One of the reasons I found it terrifying to call was I had no idea what to say. After pondering it for months, I realized I could call her and thank her. I'd let her know I was grateful for her sacrifice, for what she went through to give me life. I would comfort her and not make the call about me. I had no idea what I was looking for anyway, so this approach gave me a reason to reach out. Lee Ann said she was in tears on the phone. She was in pain. I could do this. In fact, I *should* do it. I stared at the phone in my office for over an hour, praying for the strength to pick it up, "Please God, help me. Give me courage."

The December sun was slipping away when I dialed my birth mother's number. Heart racing and hand shaking, I clutched the receiver as the phone rang four times before I got an answering machine. I hung up. Damn it! Now I had to find the courage to do it again.

Another hour went by. It was dark in my office when I picked up the phone again, my fear so liquid I could taste it. I had to use my left hand to place my right hand on the phone. I was swimming in raw animal dread. As crazy as it seems, I was afraid for my life, terrified that what was on the other end of the phone could somehow annihilate me. I took a deep breath and dialed the number again. This time, she answered.

I said, "Is this Yvette?"

She said, "Yes, who is this?"

I said, "Mary Gauthier."

She said, "Who?"

My heart sank.

She had not bothered to write down my name.

I said, "March 11, 1962."

She started to cry.

I waited.

She gathered herself and said, "Why are you calling me?"

I said, "Because I want to thank you for the gift of life, for bringing me into this world. I believe you are my mother."

She started to cry again.

I waited.

She said, "Have you had a good life?"

I almost laughed. I waited a bit.

"Umm, well, yeah. It's been a good life, like many, I guess. Good times, bad times, hard times, blessings, struggles. Glad to be here in spite of it all. Listen, Yvette, the people who adopted me were troubled. I was troubled. I left home young."

She started crying again.

"I'm fine now, clean and sober, in fact. I am doing well. I'm a survivor, a fighter. I'd really like to meet you. I'll come to where you are. Can we have lunch or something?"

She said, "I love you, but I cannot do that. It's too much. I am not ready."

I said, "Why not?"

She said, "I don't know how to tell you this, but you are a secret. No one knows about you. I never told anyone I was pregnant. I went away. No one knows what happened. I can't undo that now. I married a man a few years after I had you. He had a child from a previous marriage. I raised her. He died two years ago, and I have not been doing well, it's been so hard on me, so hard for me to carry on."

She went on, "We had a beautiful marriage, it was a wonderful marriage, we were very, very close and I don't know how to put myself back together with him gone. I have a grown kid that I raised as my own and see every day and I can't do this with you. I can't."

For a moment I floundered. I didn't know where to go from here, but then it occurred to me I could at least ask for a picture. I've always wanted to know if there's someone in this world who looked like me. I said, "Ok then, will you send me a picture? I've always wanted to know if I looked like you. It's been something that's weighed heavy on me. I was adopted by olive-skinned Italians. I do not look like anyone in my family. It would mean so much if you'd send me a picture. I feel like a stranger, an alien, not looking like anyone I know. I will send you a picture of me, ok? Do you want one? Or do you already know what I look like? Did you go to my website?"

"I don't have a computer."

"Well, you can go to the library, they have one, right?"

"I don't know how to do that."

"Well, ok, I will send you a picture of me, and you send me a picture of you? Let's start there. Then we can see what's next, ok?"

"I will."

The next day, I sent her a picture of me and a short letter thanking her for taking my call. It took weeks, but she sent me a letter and a picture. Her letter read,

Mary,

You beat me to the draw on pictures. I received yours last week. Thanks so much for sending them. I have to say you really do not look like me (or anybody I have ever known). Not sure what that means!!!!!! I'm sending you a picture of me, and the other is of my sister and me. We are both short. I have a brother. He is also short.

Love,
Yvette

In the picture, she is holding a large rectangular cake, the kind grocery stores make. The cake says in curlicue icing, "Happy Birthday."

I don't know who that cake was for, but it wasn't for me. I've always found holidays difficult, but my birthday is my least favorite day of the year.

I was starting to understand why.

Nine

MOTHER:
SONG AS PRAYER

Mother

Mother, you had me but I never had you
I wanted you but you didn't want me
So I just got to tell you goodbye, goodbye

Father, you left me but I never left you
I needed you but you didn't need me
So I just got to tell you goodbye, goodbye

Children, don't do what I have done
I couldn't walk and I tried to run
So I just got to tell you goodbye, goodbye

Mama don't go daddy come home
Mama don't go daddy come home
Mama don't go daddy come home
Mama don't go daddy come home
Mama don't go daddy come home
Mama don't go daddy come home
Mama don't go daddy come home
Mama don't go daddy come home

—John Lennon

Songs fill the air in grocery stores, salons, airports, malls, movies, cars, elevators, gas stations, restaurants, on TV, and in movies. They are unavoidable, everywhere, all the time. Most float by and nothing important happens. They stay in the background, superficial transactions. But every now and then a song makes us stop what we are doing and listen with our full attention. The "pull over to the side of the road" song functions as an emotional x-ray, it shows us our insides and makes us feel more alive. It is a spiritual engagement, not just an acoustic one. Some songs are disposable, some indispensable. There are songs, then there are *songs*.

For me, songs like Hank Williams's poetic take on loneliness "I'm So Lonesome I Could Cry," Bob Dylan's prayerful blessing "Forever Young," David Bowie's songs of alienation and estrangement like "Space Oddity" and "Life on Mars," Prince's "When Doves Cry," Stephen Foster's "Hard Times Come Again No More," Leonard Cohen's "Hallelujah," and thousands more are way more than entertainment. They are beloved prayers, little salvations. My belief in them is absolute. I wish we'd sung them in church when I was a child.

As I was working my way through writing the songs for *The Foundling*, John Lennon's "Mother" became one of those *songs*; a road map, an anchor, a prayer. "Mother" captures the emotional damage that comes from the trauma of childhood parental abandonment. Raw, naked, and brave, "Mother" screamed what I most needed to hear: there was someone who'd been where I was and made it through to the other side, someone brave enough to articulate that experience. John Lennon had stared down what I was still trying to find the courage to look at.

The lyrics to "Mother" sprang from memories he'd probably struggled to forget, but ultimately chose to summon after several months of primal scream therapy with psychotherapist Arthur Janov. In this therapy, the patient recalls and re-enacts a particularly disturbing past experience, usually one that occurred early in life, then expresses their repressed anger or frustration through unrestrained screams.

Janov said, "John's level of pain was enormous. He was almost completely non-functional. He couldn't leave the house. He could hardly leave his room . . . This was someone the whole world adored, and it didn't change a thing. At the center of all that fame and wealth and adulation was just a lonely little kid."

Determined to confront and free himself from childhood trauma, Lennon's debut solo album, *John Lennon/ Plastic Ono Band*, featured a number of self-revelatory songs inspired by his work with Janov. Songs like "Working Class Hero," "Isolation," and the chilling, monotone "My Mummy's Dead."

"Mother" was released as the first single. An unlikely, revolutionary single if there ever was one, this song contains so much pain it's hard to hear, and the desperation and primal hurt in Lennon's vocals unnerved many of his fans. Add to that the song's stark lyrics and the series of feral screams and shrieks on the song's coda, and fans were left wondering why John Lennon would put such a terrifying song out into the world.

Not me. I understood why he wrote this song and sang it the way he sang it, and I loved him for it. He did it as an expression of loyalty to his own life force. The act of making music as resistance, opposition to the pain. He did it because he had to. Making art keeps an artist's soul alive.

After playing a radio show in London and talking on air about how I was drawn to this song, I was gifted a CD of the outtakes of the "Mother" recording session by a fellow adoptee who worked for BBC Radio. "I think this will speak to you," he said. Lord, was he right.

The outtakes of "Mother" were instructive. As John searched for the best way to sing this intense song, he ran it with the band over and over, looking for the emotional center. There are several near misses, then, four or five takes in, he nails it, the keeper, the one that will make the album, a performance head and shoulders above the rest. Harrowing and primal, Lennon's vocals are guttural screams from an abandoned child. His voice sounds like a baby crying, howling. Not a performance so much as the ripping off of protective skin, John's voice is the sound of free-falling terror, a man plummeting, untethered. His savage howls shredded his vocal cords; after he sang this song he physically could not sing any more that day.

The "Mother" outtakes came to me like a message in

a bottle thirty years after John recorded them: Tell your story real, tell it true. Be courageous. Do not worry about who you will scare, who you will offend, or if it will sell. Do this for your own soul, for your own salvation. Do it because you're called to. You can't be loved if you can't be seen and heard, and you can't be seen and heard if you can't articulate what's inside of you. Do it for love, love of life, and love of self. "Mother" insisted I present *The Foundling* in full, without apology or holding back.

In "Mother," John cries over and over:

> *Mama don't go*
> *Daddy come home*

At first listen, a song like this sounds like the artist is falling apart. In reality, the opposite is happening. There is a release, a catharsis, a discharge of pent-up emotions, then, a liberation. When a secret is said aloud, it allows others to bear witness and empathize. Genuine understanding can occur, which can then make way for hard-earned peace. Art and truth can lighten the burden so that the wound can begin to heal. Art and truth help hold things together *especially* when the truths are hard. In fact, there is no need to write about things everyone can already say. The job of a songwriter is to write things that are difficult to say. It is an ancient practice, singing what we dare not say.

Listening to John Lennon sing "Mother" showed me the problem I was dealing with was not unique to me. Maternal abandonment leaves a scar. To survive it is to be shaped by it, or misshapen by it. The wound haunts you, it embeds in your shadow, your breath, your blood, your nightmares, and your dreams. I was learning this truth in my midforties, John learned it in his thirties. The effects of relinquishment can be repressed, but they cannot be outrun.

In my London hotel room, headphones on, listening to Lennon's outtakes of "Mother," it occurred to me that singing can be a powerful form of prayer. Here, then, was a man praying for release from his past with a heartbreaking sincerity. His courage in telling his story would help me tell mine. I was beginning to see that the choices I'd made in my life had been affected by what happened to me as a child. The core belief that I carried, way down, was that I was unlovable; there was something inherently wrong with me, something so hideous it made me unworthy; that's why my mother gave me away, that's why my relationships had not worked.

What to do with these feelings and beliefs? John Lennon instructs: go to the pain, stare it down, howl it out, moan, scream it back out into world. Publicly name and claim the wound, release the infection. Keep going till there is no more story to tell, then learn how to let it go.

Throughout my life, when I was deep in the ache of my own aloneness, I'd reach for music to point to emotional pathways I could walk in communion with at least one other person. The artists who bring forth longing, reveal hurt, and sing of both the beautiful and the dreadful are the artists I always turn to when I need emotional reinforcement. Those who stand emotionally naked and sing their truth, even when it is unpopular. Their willingness to stand alone, exiled, in front of the group is both gallant and courageous and inspires me to be brave, too.

St. Francis of Assisi said, "One who works with their hands is a laborer. One who works with their hands and head is a craftsman. One who works with their hands, their head and their heart is an artist."

Artists are links in a chain, rungs in a ladder that span the entirety of human history. Call it god or genius, truth or talent or love, but no matter what you call it, the thing that connects an individual to the source manifests uniquely. No two voices are the same, and every voice matters. The articulations do not need to be complex. As the great country songwriter Harlan Howard once said, a country song is three chords and the truth. Anyone who is driven to truth and self-expression can become an artist.

Lennon's talent was to talk to everyone in a simple way about the magic and tragedy of our human condition, that to become an adult, you must make peace with your parents, forgive them, and learn to let go. That said, it's the ambivalence in "Mother" that makes it so heartbreaking. The first verse is about saying goodbye, trying to say: You didn't care about me, so I don't care about you. But in the last minutes, it's about not wanting to say goodbye after all. It's one thing to understand that forgiveness and letting go are the answer, and another thing to know how to do it. Lennon instructs us: it can be done through courage, vulnerability, and art.

Ever since I started writing songs, I've been asked the question, "Does the music come first, or the words?" My answer is: there are no rules. It's different every time. I start where I can. When I can. However I can.

The starting place is irrelevant. It's clichéd, but if I knew where the great songs came from, I'd go there more often.

But here's what I do know: artists are like firemen; when the rest of the world is running away from the explosion, they run to it and report back. Artists feel the heat, touch the burn, write the thing they have to write, the particular story they are on fire for, the one that breaks their own hearts, the one that only they can tell. The ask is this: no matter how many songs you've written—each time, the struggle is to get back to that singular place where it is just you and the fire alone in the room.

Ten

SWEET WORDS: REBIRTH

Sweet Words

I don't trust my eyes any more
They don't know what they're looking for
Thinking back on what they didn't see
I think my eyes were blinding me

Some people never really love
They don't mean the sweet words they say
Other people can't see the truth
I didn't know I was that way
I didn't know I was that way

I don't trust my ears anymore
They don't know what to listen for
They don't hear the spirit for the sound
My ears only serve to bring me down

Some people never really love
They don't mean the sweet words they say
Other people can't hear the truth
I didn't know I was that way
I didn't know I was that way

I don't trust my heart anymore
It's busted open, bruised, beat up and sore

Even while it's limping round in pain
All it wants to do is reach for you again

I don't trust my eyes
I don't trust my ears
I can't trust my heart
It lied to me for years

Some people never really love
They don't mean the sweet words they say
Other people won't accept the truth
I didn't know I was that way
I didn't know I was that way

—Mary Gauthier

I was struggling, again. Another catastrophic romantic relationship had blown up in my hands, and I was shattered. A friend told me he knew a woman named Maria in New Mexico who could help. He said she was a crone healer, a white witch medicine woman who lived in an adobe outside Santa Fe. Supposedly she had worked with Dylan during one of his divorces. I called her and she said "come."

The following day, I boarded a plane for the Land of Enchantment. I imagined Maria as a New Mexican Stevie Nicks. I saw her in a layered, colorful tribal dress that billowed in the moonlight as her long raven-black hair blew off her shoulders. I pictured strong hands wrapped around a crystal ball. I imagined burning sage, ancient tarot cards, gypsy spells, and sorcery.

We met in the café at the Eldorado Hotel, Santa Fe. When she walked in wearing blue jeans, sandals, and sunglasses, I didn't know what to think. She did not look the least bit witchy. But I liked the way she moved in her long-sleeved mauve silk and lace shirt; the way she held her head high, long hair hanging down, shoulders back. She walked right up to me and said, "Mary?" She must have known who I was from the sadness on my face.

The late afternoon New Mexican sky outside the café

window was a kaleidoscope of changing colors as she smiled, reached for my hand, and held it. I leaned in. Because of her kindness, my heart enlarged in my chest, leaving me teary-eyed and exposed. I'd been raw for months, stumbling around inconsolable. "Dear God, please let this woman help me," I prayed. "Please help her bring me some kind of an answer."

We both ordered peppermint tea, and after a few quick minutes of small talk, she asked me why I'd come. I began telling my story of love, loss, confusion, and betrayal. When I stopped to take a breath, she said, "Sweetheart, I believe I know what you need."

I had more to say, but maybe this was the part where she'd light something on fire in an ashtray, or pull out tarot cards, or go into a trance?

Nope.

She said without hesitation, "My dear, you should go to the bookstore. There's a book there you must read. It's called *The Sociopath Next Door*. It will help you understand."

My heart sank. I came all the way to Santa Fe to be sent to the bookstore? She smiled, held my hands in hers again, squeezed them, and thanked me. She did not ask for money. She stood up and walked out of the café.

What to do? I walked over to the bookstore and bought the book, then I changed my flight home, packed my bag, went back to the airport, and started reading on the airplane.

The author, Martha Stout, a Harvard professor in the department of psychiatry for twenty-five years, described

sociopathy as an untreatable mental disorder. Relationships with sociopaths are endless games of emotional
manipulation and calculated domination, a sport. These
descriptions sounded painfully familiar. I recognized this
personality type, having just gotten out of a relationship
with someone whose behavior fit this description. The
shock of recognition flooded my being. The book had
my full attention. After years of relationship failures with
varying degrees of fault on both sides, it was dawning on
me that a couple of these disasters were truly dangerous.
Another passage jumped out and hit hard. "Sociopaths often marry, but never for love."

Was Maria telling me I put myself in danger? I thought
about it, and it made sense. My standards for getting in-
volved with someone included two things: Is she beautiful?
Does she like me? The feeling of safety in a relationship
had eluded me; I had no real understanding of it, yet. It
was embarrassing to admit this to myself, but at least some
of my story was starting to make sense.

I went to Provincetown, rented a room, and focused on
writing more songs for *The Foundling*. I brought *The Sociopath Next Door* with me, dog-eared, with hundreds of pas-
sages highlighted. After I settled into my room, got some
groceries, coffee, tea, sparkling water, and a candle, I sat at
the desk with my guitar and began.

I started a song I called "Sweet Words." The pain of my
breakup was finding its way into the song, but so was the
bigger foundling story. It was moving along but I got stuck

on the last line of the chorus. I played it over and over and
knew something was wrong. I'd written:

> *Some people never really love*
> *They don't mean the sweet words they say*
> *Other people can't see the truth*
> *I didn't know you were that way*

The words did not feel right in my gut. Something was
not true. I decided to take a long walk down Commercial
Street, all the way to the beach, where the land meets the
open water by the Provincetown Inn. As I stood on the
rocks thinking, the answer came. The song was not working because the focus was misguided. I thought the song
was about my former lover. I needed to flip perspective
and make it about the narrator, that is, *me*! Put it in first
person.

I went back to my room, grabbed my guitar, and
switched the last line of the chorus to, "I didn't know I was
that way."

Goosebumps.

I'd found it.

My truth.

The chorus became:

> *Some people never really love*
> *They don't mean the sweet words they say*
> *Other people can't see the truth*
> *I didn't know I was that way*

It was ME who could not see the truth. I was in my midforties and still could not trust myself enough to know what I knew, see what I saw. *I talked myself out of knowing.* The song was telling me, in a gentle but direct way, I did not yet know how to truly give or receive love.

I ended up on a healer's table in Nashville as she guided me through my origin story. The healer instructed, "We are now going to the scene of your birth," and for the first time ever, I began to imagine my beginnings. As strange as it may sound, I'd never thought of myself as actually being born, only adopted.

Eyes closed; I can see her.

"My mother is on a hard bed, or maybe a table with blanket on top, in a delivery room. She's terrified and trapped, a stranger's hands on her body. Contractions are coming fast. Breathing is difficult."

For me to be born, did a part of my mother have to die? I did not want this for her. Not at all. But she must have wanted it, *me,* gone, wanted it done, wanted it over. She may have wanted to die, wanted us to die, but I did not want to die! I suddenly know this in every cell of my body. I wanted to live. I wanted my life.

I envisioned myself born into the hands of the doctor and handed off to one of the Sisters of Charity. I probably took my first breath in the arms of a nun. I don't know if my mother held me. I don't know if she even looked at me. She simply disappeared.

The healer guided me through the process again, this time with me as my mother, giving birth to myself. She had me welcome myself to the world, tell myself I would be there for myself, always.

Four hours later, I opened my eyes and looked around the healer's office. My shirt was wet from tears, as was the table I was lying on. The first thing I saw was a painting of the Madonna and child on the office wall. I'd never liked that image. But I'd also never considered why it was so off-putting to me. Whenever I thought about Jesus the human, I saw him either as an infant in a manger staring into his mother's face for the first time or staring down from the crucifix, again into his loving mother's face, for the last time. Properly mothered, loved, from birth to death.

Looking at the Madonna and child painting now, something in me had shifted. The negative feelings had been removed. It was just a painting of a mother and a child.

In the early months of recovery from drug and alcohol addiction, my face felt pressed against a mountain of problems so high I could not see the top. I was told that the peace I longed for was on the other side, but I didn't believe I could get there. I had no understanding of where "there" was; it was anywhere but where I was, I suppose. Without even knowing it, little by slow, I had already begun to take baby steps every day up the mountain.

Songs and stories were leading me, they'd been doing it all along. I didn't know the depths of my sorrow until I wrote about it, then heard it in my music. Songwriting and recovery had led me back into my hazy past in order to grab the hand of that kid stuck in the story of abandonment. Now that I had her hand, it was time for a better story.

Spirit is bigger than parental influences or biology. It's ever unfolding. It is limitless in possibility. Spirit is the deepest truth. I had to work my way back through my beginning to find spirit waiting there for me; I'd carried it inside all along. I was closing in on a collection of songs that tell the story I was born to tell: *The Foundling*.

I was several decades sober at this point, but still, when I woke up, right before I opened my eyes, I felt an aching emptiness as though in my sleep I'd gone back to the orphanage and sat alone in my crib again, waiting, hoping that she—my mother, myself?—was coming back. I woke up haunted, would try to scrub the dread off my skin in a hot shower, but the feeling waited for me every night when I went back to sleep.

I had struggled to form connections. My attachments had been fragile, troubled. I had been looking for home since the day I was born. I may not have found home yet, but I found a missing part of myself. A foundling, a condition I compulsively returned to and defended against, the sense of being thrown out, thrown away, waiting and praying to be found. There are other words that might describe this part of me, but "foundling" is the word that sits most comfortably on my tongue. It feels most true.

At the center of my heart lived a tangled web of emotions so complex that it has taken me decades of recovery from drug and alcohol addiction as well as therapy and healers to begin to unravel the mystery that is me.

I'd found my birth mother, but she did not want to be found. I called her one last time and asked her if she would please tell me who my father was. She said she didn't remember. I knew she was lying, but I also knew she was terrified. It was time for me to let go, move on.

The road to healing demands no less than everything, but the rewards make the effort worthwhile. When we throw the lead of our personal story into the transformative fires of creativity, hardship and pain are transformed into something else, something that heals. The songs for *The Foundling* were complete.

I recorded the songs in Toronto with Michael Timmons from the Cowboy Junkies as the producer. Then, I put it out into the world. I played just those eleven songs for one solid year, in sequence, nightly, town to town, country to country, with only a violin player by my side.

I performed them as a keynote speech at the annual conference of the American Adoption Congress where I met Betty Jean Lifton and Nancy Verrier, the two authors whose books helped me to understand adoption trauma. I was able to thank them both, and to my amazement they thanked me as well. They said *The Foundling* songs would be used in therapy around the world to help members of the adoption community for years to come. I hoped that maybe my songs might do for someone what John Lennon's "Mother" had done for me.

I played the songs in London at the Foundling Museum, where I learned about the Puritan basis for the American system of closed adoption. I played them in Sydney and in

Oslo and in Stockholm and in Paris and in New York and in LA. I played them in over 150 cities and over a dozen countries.

To say I "played" those songs is a poor description for what consumed me as I presented them to audiences around the world. These songs did not make for a playful performance. Honestly, it was as hard a job as there is. I knew the songs were disturbing, I knew that they were difficult to listen to. But I was committed to the journey; I knew it was a part of my life's work. For a year, that's what I did. And when, on occasion, people reached out to catch and hold me, if only for a little while, I let them. People told me their stories: so many had their own struggles to report, adoptive parents, birth mothers, other adoptees. Their stories gave me courage, brought me strength, and kept me focused on my mission.

I'd inscribed a quote from Gregory Armstrong's "Wanderers All" on the front page of the artwork for *The Foundling* record because I knew it to be true for me.

> *All the boys and girls without fathers and mothers . . .*
> *All the little wanderers who never give up searching . . .*
> *All the strangers on earth who have lost their way.*
> *How could they know that there is no way and there never*
> *   has been?*
> *How could they know that no one ever finds their way?*
> *How could they know that there never were any mothers or*
> *   fathers?*
> *Only other little wanderers like themselves.*

When the year of touring *The Foundling* ended, I never played those songs in front of an audience again. It was time to move on.

But I had one more stop. At eighteen years sober, I checked myself into a thirty-day treatment center that dealt with love addiction and co-dependency.

Eleven

OH SOUL:
REDEMPTION

Oh Soul

Black clouds blowing 'cross a blustery sky
Black clouds blowing 'cross a blustery sky
South of Highway 7 all alone crying
Oh soul I sold you away

When you sell your soul it opens a deep dark hole
When you sell your soul it opens a deep dark hole
Drink'll leave you thirsty fire'll leave you cold
Oh soul I sold you away

Oh my soul I sold you away oh my soul I sold you away
Oh my soul I sold you away oh soul I sold you away

It started with desires sweet soft kiss
It started with desires sweet soft kiss
Ended in an alley with my face against a fist
Oh soul I sold you away

Oh my soul I sold you away oh my soul I sold you away
Oh my soul I sold you away oh soul I sold you away

Redemption, redemption have mercy on me
Redemption, redemption have mercy on me
A body's but a prison when the soul's a refugee
Oh soul I sold you away

I'm pulling into Greenwood to get down on my knees
Pulling into Greenwood to get down on my knees
By Robert Johnson's grave pray my soul back to me
Oh soul I sold you away

Oh my soul I sold you away oh my soul I sold you away
Oh my soul I sold you away oh soul I sold you away

—Mary Gauthier and Ben Glover

With the help of my therapist, I entered a treatment center outside of Santa Fe, New Mexico, Life Healing Center. The center specialized in relationship/love/sex addiction and co-dependency. My therapist described relationship addiction as "One person 'loving' another person with an obsessive intensity that is not in the best interest of either party." Her description resonated.

I hoped this treatment would bring me an understanding of why I kept failing at romantic relationships. I'd watched my friends get married, have children, build homes and families, while I repeated the same mistakes over and over. I'd not been able to maintain a relationship for more than three years.

The pattern was predictable: When a relationship ended (many times at my insistence), I would panic and beg my lover to come back. This would lead to an extended back and forth that hurt both of us more than we already were hurting. When the back and forth failed, and it always failed, I would get into a new relationship. Trapped in this awful cycle, I had to agree with my therapist. I needed to find a way out of the loop.

The treatment center van was waiting for me at the Albuquerque airport. As I walked with the driver from baggage claim to the parking lot, the white van reminded me of the last recovery van I'd ridden in twenty-five years prior as a fifteen-year-old kid on the way to a halfway house in Salina, Kansas, a lifetime ago. We loaded my suitcase and guitar, and I sat in the back seat. Once we were on the highway, the driver caught my eye in the rearview and asked me if I was THE Mary Gauthier.

Oh boy, here we go.

I nodded yes.

He said he was a fan. He'd seen me play at the Thirsty Ear Festival outside Santa Fe, said it was wonderful to meet me. I smiled, thanked him, felt embarrassed, and looked down. There was no way to gloss over where this van was headed. He spent the rest of the trip in merciful silence.

We pulled into the treatment center compound, and a counselor met me at the front desk, greeted me with a smile, said, "Hi, I'm Karen. Welcome!"

I filled out the paperwork. Karen asked for my phone. I handed it to her. She said I could use it once daily for twenty minutes in the office, supervised. Then, she locked it in a box.

I signed a pile of papers. They took my vitals, then Karen walked me, my suitcase, and my guitar across campus to the women's house. Heads turned; everyone was checking out the new ward.

Patients wore street clothes. The men sat smoking and sulking on picnic benches with other men; the women sat across the quad with other women.

Segregated by sex.

There were no smiles, no "welcome to the loony bin, comrade" nods from either camp. Karen told me that women and men were not allowed to talk to each other here, except in shared group twice a week. Breaking this rule was grounds for dismissal. I thought this made sense for heterosexuals but was a bizarre rule for gay people. I kept my mouth shut, but I was not thrilled.

Men were my friends, my mentors, my buddies— guys like Gurf Morlix, Darrell Scott, Crit Harmon, Fred Eaglesmith, Ray Wylie Hubbard, Bob Neuwirth, Ralph Murphy, Guy Clark, and David Olney. My relationship with them was about music, respect, admiration. I felt safe around them, protected. It's not that I don't have women friends. I do! It's just that for most of my life, after I got sober, I found men safe, and easy to be around. My relationships with women have been far more nuanced and complicated.

I know that my presence has confused many a heterosexual woman who found herself drawn to me. This never happens with straight men. Straight men are not attracted to me because they almost always go for much more outwardly feminine-looking women.

Karen walked me and my suitcase and guitar through the front door, down the hall, and into my closet-sized single room. She put my suitcase on the twin bed and went through my belongings. Slowly. Carefully. With a fine-toothed comb.

I asked, "What are you looking for? There's no dope. I've been sober eighteen years."

She smiled politely but continued pulling everything out and putting it on the twin bed. She had my toiletry bag open now and was dismantling it item by item. She pulled my fingernail clippers out, put them in a bag she pulled out of her pocket, and said, "No sharps."

"Sharps?"

"We don't allow fingernail files, fingernail clippers, razors, or any kind of knives on campus."

"Why?"

"Patients have used them in the past to self-harm."

Well, damn it, there went my sharps. Fingernail clippers, nail file, razor, all gone. I needed my nail clippers and file to keep my nails short to play guitar. I'd never been a day without them. I suddenly resented every self-harmer who'd come through the doors, then felt bad for thinking that way. This was going to be a long month.

Karen finished going through my bags and said, "Well, that does it. You'll get your sharps back when you leave. Welcome! Group is at 3:30; it's 1:30 now, so you have two hours of free time. See you at group!"

"Yeah. Ok. Thanks."

I was not excited about "free time."

I sat on the flammable-looking synthetic ocean blue comforter on my twin bed and looked at my sharp-less belongings. Then I decided to walk around and have a look at what I'd gotten myself into.

The house had six bedrooms, one bathroom. Mine was the only room with one bed. Most rooms were double or triple occupancy.

I went to the living room and sat on the couch.

A tall, leggy young woman with high cheekbones, pouty lips, and very short shorts walked through the front door with a basket of laundry. I'd seen her from the corner of my eye when I checked in. She looked like a super-model. I thought I recognized her face from the cover of some magazine. I'd seen her checking me out as I checked in; I saw her look at my guitar. She introduced herself. "Hi. I'm Raz. You're new, huh? You a musician?"

"Yeah, I write songs," I said.

She put down the laundry basket and sat next to me on the couch. She flashed a megawatt smile and said she'd been in this place for ten days. Her boyfriend Jim was the lead singer for a famous rock band and currently in rehab in Arizona. She was extremely friendly, leaning in like she knew me. She said she didn't think she had a problem with sex, love, or co-dependency, and she wasn't sure why she was in this awful fucking place.

She moved off the couch, sat on the floor, and kept talking.

I stayed on the couch.

She became more and more animated as she talked. She moved her hands and body in a kind of up-and-down motion. Then she sprang up, grabbed a yoga ball from the corner of the living room, rolled it to the middle of the floor, sat on it, and began slowly bouncing her butt up and down on it. She kept her eyes on me and talked as she bounced.

She was hot.

I was screwed.

This was what could only be called . . . a rough start. I

hadn't been in sex/love/co-dependency treatment for an hour, and I was already feeling the fire again. But for once, I did not want to be the target of a beautiful woman's gyrations. I didn't want to feel what I was feeling. I began to get angry.

Raz ran up to her room and came running down with a DVD in her hand. She said, "I want to show you a video of me and Jim singing!" She popped in the music video she'd made with her rock star boyfriend and cranked it. She was topless, so was he. They were making out on a blanket on a cliff near a beach, dripping wet from swimming in the ocean. Drums pounded. Guitars wailed.

This soft porn "music" video, this woman's focused attention, it was all too much. I jumped up, told her I had to meet Karen back at the office, and got the hell out of there.

Karen was in a meeting. I sat down in the hallway outside her office and waited for her. When she came out, I grabbed her, "This is not going to work. I cannot stay in the women's house. Putting me in a house full of women to work on sex and love addiction and co-dependency is like putting a dope fiend in a pharmacy to kick dope. Either put me in the men's house, or I'm out. I can't do this."

Karen smiled and put her arm around me.

It seemed we were buddies, now?

She said, "Mary, perhaps you could slow down a little? Let's take a little walk, shall we?"

She walked me around campus, away from the other patients sitting at picnic tables smoking, and we talked. I told her what had transpired in the living room of the women's house.

She said, "You're making a lot of assumptions. Let me break this down for you, ok?"

We sat down on a bench. She looked at me with kindness and asked me what I felt as Raz did her thing on the ball. I was ashamed to say it. But I told her.

She said addiction is not a manifestation of love but rather more closely associated with lust. She said I would learn I had choices; all this would make sense to me soon. I was in the right place. There were very good reasons for me to remain in the women's house.

I said ok, I'll think about it.

We walked back to the women's house. I went to my room, closed the door, sat on the twin bed, and prayed. "Please show me what I'm supposed to do. Please help me accept your answer. Thy will, not mine be done."

A bell rang.

It was time for Women's Daily Integrity Group. There were five women in the circle. Raz was not there. It was my first check-in, but when my turn came, I let loose.

I said, "I'm Mary," then I spilled my guts. I said I felt angry and confused. Having Raz do her thing on the yoga ball made me think I should leave. I said I wasn't sure the women's house was the right place for me.

Two of the women nodded their heads yes, and one woman shared that she felt Raz was dangerous to everyone in the house.

Were they feeling what I was feeling?

As group was wrapping up, from the corner of my eye I saw Raz being walked to the van in the parking lot with her suitcase.

As I watched the van pull out, I decided I would do my full thirty days here. I would try to learn what this place could teach me. I felt bad for Raz but realized that this was the first time I'd ever resisted intrigue and seduction.

As treatment went on, I learned that the come-on dance made me feel worthy when I really felt undesirable. Intrigue made me feel chosen, selected and special. I was self-medicating, again. I needed to learn how to deal with emotional pain in some other way.

My first big crush on a straight woman was when I was fifteen, the next one was when I was sixteen living in a halfway house basement. Both women went on to marry men, as did many of my lovers after them. I believed taking straight women as lovers made me almost magical and uniquely powerful. It had not occurred to me that it was wildly self-destructive to become emotionally attached to someone believing I had the power to somehow change her. Even more insane was the belief that each new lover was THE ONE. I secretly believed each woman I slept with was my one true love who would make me whole. I did not address my own needs because I had no idea what they were (aside from the need to not be alone). I ignored or denied red flags in order to get the love I thought would save me. I had no idea how to set boundaries or how to create safety for myself.

In retrospect, it was no surprise that my relationship cycles were growing shorter, as the swinging door swung harder and faster every year. My acute emotional anguish was becoming a near constant because "love" addiction was progressive, just like the drug and alcohol addiction I'd surrendered to eighteen years prior. Until I got the lesson, it was going to keep getting worse.

I used to think naming "lust" as one of the seven deadly sins was ridiculous. I didn't think that anymore. I was fifty years old and learning that I had another monkey on my back.

In my work at Life Healing Center, I learned even more about the effects my childhood trauma had on me. The therapists diagnosed me as having disrupted attachment disorder, and I finally had a name for that aching emptiness I could never fill.

They put me into daily EMDR (eye movement desensitization and reprocessing), a psychotherapy treatment that was originally designed by the military to alleviate the distress associated with traumatic memories. It helped.

A guest therapist came in twice a week to do afternoon sessions. Her expertise was experiential work with dolls. I resisted at first because, well, DOLLS, but eventually I agreed to do it, and to my surprise, it became one of the more effective parts of my treatment.

I played out the psychodrama with other members of my group and the dolls over several sessions, till one afternoon, EUREKA! I got it. The reason I always felt abandoned was that I was abandoning MYSELF. My turmoil and struggle were not because I picked the wrong people. I did, of course, but it was not their fault.

I was drawn to women who were emotionally unavailable. If I had a partner who actually was all in, I'd leave her. I had no idea I was doing this. I could now see that the belief that I had a bad picker was a justification of my own behavior and patently false. It was a delusion, similar to the delusion that I could deal with my drinking problem by switching from whiskey to wine, deal with my heroin problem by switching to weed. The good news was that if the problem was inside me, I could deal with it.

When it was time for me to leave, I signed an exit contract and agreed to a year of sexual and romantic abstinence. I made a commitment to learn to be with myself and give myself the time I needed to work through the pain of low self-esteem and fear of abandonment, essentially, to learn how to be with myself and find peace. I felt armed and ready to face the world.

One year of abstinence became five. I stayed single and didn't date. You can't start the healing till you stop the bleeding, and this became my time to heal. I healed, I grew, I learned.

Then, I wrote and released another concept album, called *Trouble & Love*, a collection of songs about a breakup and transformation. At the center of this transformation is love, but not the kind of love that's celebrated on pop charts. In those songs, love is its own end; the story stops as giddiness sets in, with no hint of what may follow. The kind of love in *Trouble & Love* was about hard-earned self-love, dignity, and self-respect.

I started the song "Oh Soul" in my writing room in Nashville with my friend, Irish songwriter Ben Glover, who had recently visited the gravesite(s) of the blues legend Robert Johnson, in Greenwood, Mississippi. As with all things Robert Johnson, the site of his burial is mysterious, and there are several markers where he was allegedly buried, and a thorough pilgrimage requires visiting all of them. As we worked on the song, we let it talk to us.

The narrator was in pain, remembering, reeling from a betrayal but slowly coming to grips with the sad truth: she'd sold her soul and needed to find a way to get it back. In my mind, the narrator is both me and a distant cousin of the bluesman Robert Johnson, who'd famously sold his soul to the devil at a crossroads in Mississippi in a Faustian bargain for musical greatness and sway with the ladies. Legend has it that the blues singer could possess women and have any woman he wanted. In the end, the bargain killed him, because the devil never pays up.

Ben and I finished the song on the road in Denmark when, during a soundcheck, these lines came pouring into my head:

> *It started with desire's sweet soft kiss*
> *Ended in an alley with my face against a fist*
> *Oh soul I sold you away*

It was clear that the character was aware of her transgression, in search of redemption. In the last verse, we picked up the thread of the Robert Johnson legend and had the character driving down Highway 7, headed to Greenwood, Mississippi, to stand in front of Robert Johnson's grave and pray for redemption.

It was a fitting ending.

Twelve

RIFLES & ROSARY BEADS: TRANSFORMATION

Rifles & Rosary Beads

Rifles and Rosary Beads
You hold on to what you need
Vicodin morphine dreams
Rifles and Rosary Beads

Yellow smoke orange haze
Blowing into my eyes
Whistling sunset bombs
I couldn't trust the sky

Rifles and Rosary Beads
You hold on to what you need
Vicodin morphine dreams
Rifles and Rosary Beads

White knuckles wrapped around
A darkness that has no sound
Bombed out schools and homes
Kids in the streets alone

Mirrors frighten me
I don't recognize what I see
A stranger with blood on his hands
Brother, I'm not that man

Rifles and Rosary Beads
You hold on to what you need
Vicodin morphine dreams
Rifles and Rosary Beads

Rifles and Rosary Beads
You hold on to what you need

—Mary Gauthier and Joe Costello

In 2013, twenty years and eight records into my songwriting career, I was invited to participate in a retreat that paired professional songwriters with wounded veterans and their families. Mary Judd and Darden Smith, co-founders of the non-profit SongwritingWith:Soldiers (SW:S), started the program after Darden and his friend, fellow songwriter Radney Foster, wrote the incredible song "Angel Flight" with an active-duty soldier. During that process Darden saw how powerful the pairing of songwriters and soldiers could be.

SW:S retreats usually involve four professional songwriters, six to ten veterans, sometimes their families, several volunteers, a therapist, and a cook. We gather on Friday night, share a meal, then get to work. By Sunday afternoon, eight to ten new songs will have emerged.

Our job as songwriters is to help turn the veterans' stories into songs. The songwriter brings decades of songwriting experience, the veteran brings their story. Before I worked my first retreat, I assumed that asking a wounded soldier to open up to a songwriter would be a stretch. I'd heard that silence is the soldier's code; that those who have seen combat do not talk about it, those who talk about it have not seen it. Coming out the other side alive is enough. Soldiers talk to soldiers if they talk at all. But I quickly learned that when a veteran feels seen and heard, not assessed, judged, or evaluated, they open up and help the songwriter turn their story into a song that allows others to see and hear them. This happens not by trying to write a "healing" song but through the vulnerability of emotional honesty. In this way, the dominant narrative of war trauma can be written into a universal story that many can relate to, even those who have no knowledge or experience of the military. The song can also become a step beyond the self, toward others who perhaps have felt the same way. A powerful transformation can occur when this happens. I knew this from personal experience, from how my own songs had transformed me.

Some of the veterans do not really want to be at the retreat. They come because they don't know what else to do. Someone who cares suggested it: their therapist or the VA, their wife, their pastor. They show up unsure and in pain. I see it on their faces during that first meal on Friday night, some are thinking, "This kumbaya crap might be an all-time low, how in the hell is a song going to help me?"

My job is to sit with a veteran, just the two of us, in a quiet place, and ask them questions. How are you doing? Where do you live? When did you serve? Where? What branch of the military? Are you still active duty, or retired? We start talking. I ask them, "Is there anything you might want to write about?"

Before long, they start to tell me their story, little by slow. I play a little music on my guitar, find a melody that matches what they're saying. The music helps open them up; a sympathetic melody is like a magnet that pulls their story out. They feel seen and heard, which helps them feel safe. If it all goes well, we will create a song that is a mirror reflection of their soul, something the veteran can point to and say, "This. This is me. My song. This is how I feel."

Songs float in on the wings of a benevolent mystery to help humans with life struggles. If you choose to approach songwriting as a spiritual practice, it becomes one. What is a "spiritual practice"? I think of it as a practice that actively works on a relationship with Spirit. Mine and yours. Songwriting as a spiritual practice is rooted in a constant effort to be more charitable. There's a spirit inside us that leans toward love like a flower to the sun, a built-in mechanism that pushes us toward connection. When I think of spirituality, this is what I imagine.

"The primary function of the human brain is to be in sync with other brains," says my friend Dr. Bessel van der Kolk, renowned psychiatrist and post-traumatic stress expert. Even the most harrowing stories, in the end, are about love, or lack of love. It's the same for everyone, even the toughest of the tough guys—most of life's joy comes from love and connection, and most pain comes from love lost. Romantic love, yes, but even more importantly empathy, both given and received. Love is what saves us.

Veterans' songs inevitably end up as prayers for peace. This is not the result of an allegiance to a particular agenda. It happens naturally as the song emerges, as we sit in discomfort together, working, waiting for the truth to appear. The songwriter bears witness in non-judgment, and we write what we hear the veteran saying.

My first veteran co-write was with two female soldiers,

Meaghan and Brittney, at a retreat center outside of Austin, Texas. After initial hellos and small talk, we got down to business. I noticed that these two veterans sat next to each other, whispered in each other's ear, occasionally held each other's arm. I asked them to tell me about their friendship. "Did y'all serve together? Were y'all battle buddies?"

They looked at me and said, "We have each other's six."

"What's that?" I asked.

They were surprised I'd never heard the term before.

"You know," one soldier said, without emotion, "I've got her back. She's got mine."

"On the battlefield," she explained, "12 o'clock is directly front of you, 6 o'clock directly behind you. To have someone's six is to have their back. 'I've got your six' means they've got you covered so the enemy can't come up behind your back and kill you. It's a declaration of loyalty."

When the full weight of what she was saying hit me, I knew I was entering another world, one I knew nothing about. To have someone's six means you'd be willing to die for them and they for you. In the soldier's world, people must be willing to die for one another, it's the only way to live. As they talked, I also understood that a part of their deep bond was survivor's guilt, the aching memory of those they'd lost. They carried the weight of that daily.

They talked and I listened, watching their body language, noting the rise and fall of their voices. I took in the stories they told as well as the ones they could not fully articulate. We sat together for a couple hours. I took notes. It got late and we called it a night. I went to my room and tried to mold what they said into a song. I did my best to make sure it conveyed what they felt and believed.

I played it for them the next morning. They liked it but pointed out a few spots where my words were not exactly right. We kept working. They added new ideas. After a few more changes, we had it. I asked them to close their eyes, sit back, and listen.

When I played their song for them from start to finish, their eyes opened wide and their jaws dropped. Watching their wonder as they heard their song for the first time, I shared in their delight. Being fully heard and having your truth mirrored back to you in a song is a powerful emotional experience. We'd written a simple song that reflected some of their most complex feelings, and a sense of kinship, even love, had emerged. "The opposite of trauma is communication," says Dr. van der Kolk.

For the first half of my life, I second-guessed my perceptions. I learned to do this early on, to survive. I was easily talked out of what I believed to be true. I learned from painful experience after painful experience that when you can't trust your own grasp of reality and set boundaries to protect yourself, you are not safe.

Watching soldiers' faces light up in awe at the power of songs that told their truth was a trip back to the beginning for me, a full-circle experience. My songs helped me become real to myself, be witnessed, and then become a witness. They saved me. Now, I was able to do this work with others, and the feeling it left me with was pure joy.

At another SW:S retreat a few months later, I was paired

up to write with a young veteran named Joe. Joe served in the Army in Iraq. Joe and I sat together in a well-lit room and started talking. He had difficulty with eye contact, his face was gaunt, his mouth set in a line. He was thirty but looked fifty. After struggling to put into words what he felt, he said, "I don't know how to explain how I feel except to say my soul hurts." Then he looked down.

There was a long silence. I waited, let the silence linger. I tried to take in the bigness of what he'd just told me. Throughout the retreat Joe had removed himself from the group, standing to the side, sitting alone. He was deeply sad.

I asked him to tell me what he saw when he got to Iraq. I asked for pictures, a slide show of what he remembered. Tell me what it was like for a nineteen-year-old kid from Austin, fresh out of boot camp, boots on the ground in a war zone for the first time.

He described yellow smoke and orange haze, bombed-out schools and homes. Kids crying in the street, alone. Soldiers with white knuckles gripping their rifles tightly, other soldiers rolling rosary beads in circles in their fingers, over and over again, praying. As he spoke, he offered to read me a poem he'd written. It included the phrase "Rifles and Rosary Beads." I suggested we write a song with that title. He liked the idea.

Then I asked him how he deals with the painful soul feeling he described, how other servicemembers deal with that. He told me everyone has their own way of dealing. His way was sometimes Vicodin. I nodded. Yeah, I said, yeah. I understand that.

We worked hard over the next two hours. I kept my voice soft, made no judgments whatsoever. I mirrored what he said, repeated his words back to him. I witnessed his pain, listened to his story, wrote his words down. I let him know I was there to work for him. He was ultimately in charge of what went into his song, he had the final say. Slowly, his detached posture began to change. His demeanor shifted. He started making eye contact, nodding his head yes when I got it right, speaking in fuller sentences and leaning toward me. He became engaged.

I asked him more questions. I made his answers rhyme and sang them back to him with a melody that matched the meaning and sounded like the feelings he described. He nodded faster as the song developed. His eyes lit up, and his lips, which had been firmly set the entire weekend, began to ease into a small, shy smile. When I missed the meaning of what he was saying he corrected me. This opened him up to tell new stories, express new feelings.

We reached a point where what he was saying became overwhelming. Hearing Joe's pain was painful to me. It hurt me to be in the presence of so much hurt. Tears began to burn behind my eyes. I told him I needed a minute, put my guitar aside, put my head in my hands, and I broke down. When I looked up, Joe was crying too. He asked if he could hug me. I nodded yes and reached for him, and we embraced. We let the intense emotion move through us, regained composure, and went back to work—mutually determined to get this song written, no matter what.

When I felt we had nailed it, I asked him to sit back and close his eyes. I played him his song, softly. After the last note rang out, his whole body relaxed in relief. His face now looked as if time had reversed itself. The deep lines on his brow had softened, the weight around his eyes lightened. He actually looked more alive.

I asked him how he was feeling. He had new tears in his eyes and said he just wanted to hug me again. I closed my computer, put down my guitar, opened my arms, and we embraced. He hugged me tight, like a child. I don't remember ever feeling more like a mother. In this moment I loved this young man with all my heart and wanted nothing more than for him to find peace.

The song we'd written had broken through walls of isolation and gave him a small ray of hope. He'd been seen, heard. He was not alone. We'd written his emotional truth, created something real he could hold on to, a small rung on the ladder to help him pull himself up out of a black hole. "Rifles & Rosary Beads" is an intense song, a sad song; Joe's story is tough. Nonetheless, we high-fived, laughed, and did a little touchdown dance when the last note rang out. It was a beautiful, joyful moment.

That night, everyone at the retreat gathered in the living room, and the songwriters played the songs that were written that day. When it came time for me to play "Rifles & Rosary Beads," I looked over at Joe as I introduced his song in front of the larger group.

As I spoke, Joe's jaw was set, his teeth clenched again, his eyes staring out at nothing.

He was terrified.

He'd been vulnerable in the co-write, exposing his deepest fears, and some of his shame had leaked into the song. I could see from his demeanor that he was worried. Trauma always brings shame, the sense of personal failure at being unable to prevent what had happened. I think of trauma as anything a person perceives as potentially annihilating, but trauma is not only what happened to you, it is what happens inside you as a result of what happened to you. The fear of exposure is anxiety producing.

As Joe braced himself in his chair waiting for me to play his song, I could see the terror of being annihilated surging through his entire being, again. It was heartbreaking to watch, but I knew that awful feeling would pass after I played the song. I knew that when a trauma story is dislodged, it releases some of the infection. To heal a wound, you must clean it first, expose it to the stinging air, allow others to witness the blood and pain. This can be the most difficult part, but it is far better than letting the infection deepen and spread.

I thought, Hang on, Joe!

I played "Rifles & Rosary Beads" for the group. After the last note rang out, instead of rejecting him—which was probably what he feared the most—the other veterans came up to him, looked him in the eyes, and thanked him, as I knew they would. They wrapped their arms around his shoulder and told him they could relate to every word. They said, "Me too, man. Me too."

Once again, I saw the power of a sad song to make a human being happy. This sad song became a balm to the wounded soul of a soldier suffering a moral injury, an injury to his conscience that had produced profound emotional guilt and shame.

Joe now had a huge smile on his face and was high-fiving the folks around him. The shape of his face had changed. He was beaming.

Storytellers have power; they are not voiceless victims. In a song we are given the authority to be the writer of the story instead of the paper it is written on. We become the narrator instead of the narrated, turning our story into something that might be useful for others. The empathy the song generates connects the songwriter to their own pain in a new way, a way that is reparative, rewiring broken circuits. Also, and this is very important, the storyteller can shape the ending, moving the story forward in a brave new way.

Trauma is removal. Removal from one's true self, removal from others. So many of the veterans I've written with just want to go home, but they don't know how to get back there. There's no longer a map. There are no words for how they feel, no way to explain their pain.

The road home is paved in human connection, and it happens in small and safe communities, where you know you are not alone. Turns out, this is what songs do best. They show our insides on the outside, reveal secrets, and demonstrate that we humans are more or less all in the same boat. Being witnessed in all our vulnerability locks in a new connection to self and others. We are not our stories, but after trauma, we often do not know that. People are not made of only the best or the worst thing we've ever done, or the best or the worst thing that has ever happened to us. A song can be the beginning of genuine hope and, sometimes, the difference between life and death.

I asked a veteran who'd been through the SW:S program, my friend Rachel Kennon, why the co-writing of her song was powerful for her. She explained. "Most military people, particularly those of us who join very young, tend to have difficulty expressing ourselves. We are trained to suck it up, don't complain, always put the mission and the team first."

She went on, "When you add trauma on to that (we both know trauma is indescribable) it exacerbates the situation. It just leaves us mute."

Rachel said her song gave voice to words she would have never been capable of saying in a million years. She said, "I still can't say those words 'I love you; I hate you' but I can sing the song. And these words were what I needed to say. It's what I actually felt."

She said, "There is a relief, a deep letting go, that results from finding a way to tell a story when you can't actually verbalize it. It's like holding your breath underwater. It actually gets to the point that it's physically painful. You just need to breathe, but you can't. It's frustrating and stressful. And then you suddenly surface and take in that first big breath. It's that kind of relief; it's lifesaving. I imagine it's similar to the moment Helen Keller discovered she could learn sign language. Can you imagine? You have no language and are trapped inside your head with your thoughts, completely isolated, then suddenly you have a way to release that. You're reborn into the world. It's the best feeling."

She said, "As veterans, we are driven to serve others, so putting our experiences into a song that could potentially help someone else also helps us. We want to be of service. Being heard by others is important; knowing other people understand how you feel and have been through similar experiences helps. All of it helps. But ultimately it's breaking the human experience in all its complexity down into a small number of words, put to a melody so others can relate to it easily. It's so simple. I was lost but now I'm found . . . ya know? I can breathe now. And once you're able to breathe again you can focus on other things. While you're underwater holding your breath, it's the only thing you can think about. It's all consuming. We need you songwriters to help us surface and breathe. We need you to help us learn to speak again."

My experience with Joe and Rachel and Josh and Meaghan and Brittney and dozens of other soldiers has left me with the pressing question: Why must anyone "soldier on" in silence when we now know doing so is destructive and dangerous? Also, the families of those who've served have a story to tell, a story that is every bit as important as the story of those who have served.

We were able to capture some of what the family goes through in a song I co-wrote called "The War After the War." Fellow songwriter Beth Nielsen Chapman worked with me, along with a group of six military spouses of different ages whose partners served at different times and in different branches of the military.

As a woman started to speak, I saw how one person's courage brought forth courage in another person, and soon enough, the stories poured out of all of them. What Beth and I heard them saying was, "He lived through it—but now we live with it." It's not only those who have served who have internalized this need to "soldier on" in silence.

Turns out, these women had plenty to say about their experience of being married to a servicemember if asked in a way that was non-judgmental, in an environment that was comfortable, respectful, and supportive. I learned quickly that when one member of a family serves, the whole family serves. Sacrifice and the effects of war affect each and every family member. As we worked, those wives embraced each other's words and stories, and when I played their song in front of the group that night, they held each other's hands and had tears streaming down their faces. The relief they experienced from the empathy they received was written all over their bodies.

Trauma, and all of its repercussions, is not limited to military personnel who have seen combat and their families. Parental neglect and abandonment; emotional, physical, and sexual abuse; assault; domestic violence; bullying; police brutality; natural or manmade disasters; medical trauma . . . the list of shockwaves is long and troubling. We are a brutal species capable of unspeakable cruelty; we are a loving species capable of great empathy and compassion, and we are caught in an age-old struggle between these two mighty truths. Many experts say trauma is likely a root cause of addiction and much of the violence in the world. Hurt people hurt people, and this cycle of violence threatens the very planet we live on. In many health care professionals' opinions trauma is our most urgent public health issue.

We need each other. We are lost without each other.

Because songs help express and transform emotional blows so low that their frequencies reverberate for a lifetime and are passed on to future generations, music and song are not just products for a marketplace. They are spiritual medicine for a world gone wrong. They can help reset the balance in favor of hope, freedom, human connection, and love. They have the power to remind us that beyond the horrifying events that have plagued human history, beyond the nightmarish legacy of wars and hate and violence and abuse, love abides.

And yet, as I sit at my desk in Nashville, I'm surrounded on all sides by music as a business and songs as products. The commercial music business's job is to extract as much money from songs as the market will allow. Songs climb the popular charts and make billions for multinational corporations. Opportunistic creators sometimes craft them with cynical intentions—music as a drug, songs as addictive meaningless confections, where the "idea" of what you are has become more important than what you actually are. The corporate takeover of every aspect of the music business has been very bad for art. Which is to say, for truth. Still, I believe in the power of song to transform a life. I've seen it over and over again.

I lived it.

When emotional truth is the goal, and courage is part of the equation, the process is deeply therapeutic, but it's not therapy.

It is the making of art.

Thirteen

STILL ON THE RIDE: TRIUMPH

Still on the Ride

Looking back now who the hell knows
Where the soul of a dead soldier goes
Guardian angels maybe they're true
My guardian angel maybe it's you

I shouldn't be here you shouldn't be gone
But it's not up to me who dies and who carries on
I sit in my room and I close my eyes
Me and my guardian angel we're still on the ride

Got holes in my eardrums, bruises and clots
Double vision, my stomach's in knots
Got pain in my fingers I hurt from head to my toes
I wake up feeling like I'm 90 years old

I shouldn't be here you shouldn't be gone
But it's not up to me who dies and who carries on
I sit in my room and I close my eyes
Me and my guardian angel, we're still on the ride

You were my brother, you were more than a friend
You were family to me right up to the end
You're still with me now I feel you, I know
You're pushing me forward and you'll never let go

I shouldn't be here you shouldn't be gone
But it's not up to me who dies and who carries on
I sit in my room and I close my eyes
Me and my guardian angel, we're still on the ride

—Mary Gauthier and Josh Geartz

I was honored to be asked to perform two songs at the Grand Ole Opry's ninetieth birthday celebration at the Ryman Auditorium. The Opry is the longest-running radio broadcast in U.S. history, performed in front of a live theater audience in Nashville, Tennessee. I chose to play "Still on the Ride" and "Mercy Now." It was a big night with a packed, sold-out house. I brought a friend along to play harmonica with me: Iraq war combat veteran Josh Geartz, my co-writer of the song "Still on the Ride." Josh suffered traumatic brain injury in Iraq, where his Humvee was destroyed and his spine was twisted, the result of a horrific IED explosion. He ended up in a wheelchair, unable to walk.

Josh flew to Nashville the day before our Opry show, thanks to Veterans Airlift Command, a volunteer group that provides free air transportation to post-9/11 combat wounded and their families for medical and other compassionate purposes through a national network of volunteer aircraft owners and pilots. Veterans Airlift Command generously flew him and his motorized wheelchair to Nashville from Buffalo, along with fellow veteran and SW:S co-writer Rob Spohr.

At Josh's request, we did a practice run after they got settled into their hotel rooms, walking and wheeling from their downtown hotel through Printers Alley to the back of the Ryman to make sure Josh's wheelchair would fit through all the doors and hallways. It did. It was all systems go, and we went to dinner excited about the following night's show.

Backstage, waiting to be called onto the Opry stage, we were hanging out in the Minnie Pearl green room. Minnie Pearl was a beloved American country comedian who appeared at the Grand Ole Opry for more than fifty years (from 1940 to 1991) and on the television show *Hee Haw* from 1969 to 1991. The green room named after her is a comfortable room right next to the stage.

Josh had gone shopping and showed up that night in a new red cowboy shirt, black cowboy boots, and his signature U.S. Army cap. When the stage manager gave us a five-minute warning, we made our way to the side of the stage and looked out into the sold-out Ryman Auditorium.

"Well, this is it, lil' bro'," I said. "Here we go. You are about to play the Grand Ole Opry!" He looked up at me from under his cap, grinned, and gave me a thumbs up.

Whispering Bill Anderson introduced me, then introduced Josh. "Ladies and gentlemen, please also welcome Retired Army Sergeant Josh Geartz, the co-writer of the next song." As I expected, the sight of Josh wheeling out in his badass six-wheeled, all-terrain wheelchair, Army cap on, harmonica and harmonica mic in hand, made the audience go wild. They welcomed him with cheers and whistles. He grinned from under his cap, nodded a shy thank-you, and we began.

I sang the first four lines, Josh played harmonica, and

the room instantly became electrically charged. I looked into the audience, and I could see people in the front rows react with deep emotion.

> *Looking back now, who the hell knows?*
> *Where the soul of a dead soldier goes*
> *Guardian angels, maybe they're true*
> *My guardian angel, maybe it's you*

Josh sat in his wheelchair on stage right, harmonica and hand-held mic in his hands. As I sang the words of the first chorus with the Opry singers adding harmonies and vocal volume, I felt an even deeper energetic tightening of the room.

> *I shouldn't be here you shouldn't be gone*
> *But it's not up to me who dies and who carries on*
> *I sit in my room, and I close my eyes*
> *Me and my guardian angel, we're still on the ride*

The sold-out Ryman audience, the Opry musicians, and house ushers were mesmerized by the power of Josh's story. The audience and the musicians were in sync, emotionally connected. I glanced down at the front row again and saw men fighting back tears, transfixed.

I'd first met Josh two years earlier at a place called the Carey Institute for Global Good, a retreat center outside Albany. That's where we wrote "Still on the Ride."

He showed up on a cold winter day with his wife, Lisa, and his service dog, Coda. I was in my bedroom looking out the window when they arrived. It was snowing. I watched as Josh angrily pushed himself up an icy hill in his old manual wheelchair, struggling with Coda's leash, Lisa by his side, hands off. I could see from the way she walked she knew he did not want her help.

The minute I first laid eyes on Josh, I knew I wanted to write with him. I just felt it, way deep inside. There was something utterly compelling about his stubbornness and defiant anger. I guess he reminded me of myself.

We were paired up the next day and went to work in a small library beside a wood-burning fireplace that I kept lit. As we talked, Josh struggled to tell one story to its conclusion before starting another. He was carrying so much trauma and pain his thoughts were like scrambled eggs. Years of battling blood clots, spinal and brain injuries, PTSD, and partial paralysis had taken their toll. I didn't know it at the time, but he had attempted suicide weeks prior and had settled on the date when he would attempt it again.

I could see that it was not his physical injuries that troubled him most; no, he was tormented most of all by survivor's guilt, having lost his best friend in a horrific crash. He said, "I shouldn't be here, he shouldn't be gone," and it gave me an idea.

I asked him if he believed in guardian angels, those mysterious benevolent beings I'd somehow managed to have faith in for my entire life, particularly in moments of great pain and revelation.

He said, "I dunno. I mean, why not?"

I asked him if he thought maybe his best friend was his guardian angel, perhaps that's why he is still here. Didn't it make sense that a dead soldier would want to continue to serve their loved ones from the spirit world? Wouldn't a dead soldier make a truly fierce guardian angel?

He thought for a moment, then looked out the window. He later told me he saw three rocking chairs on the porch, and the one in the middle had started rocking.

He looked back and nodded, "Why not? I can't think of any other reason why I'm still on the ride." I heard "Still on the Ride" as a possible title for our song, Josh agreed, and from there, we were able to write the song quickly.

KABOOM, the Opry house band drums and bass crashed in as the Opry singers added gorgeous harmonies and layers to the emotion of the first chorus, setting up the fiddle solo. The fiddle player stepped forward and made a glorious sound with her wood, strings, and bow, pressing into the emotion hard, expressing the will to live and the urgency of the need to believe. Her solo raised the hairs on my arms and nearly lifted the ceiling off of the Ryman; uplifting, defiant, and hopeful in the face of trauma and loss. The glorious sound turbo-charged my heart with adrenaline and joy. I looked over at Josh, wireless mic and harmonica between his hands, and he looked back and smiled from under his Army hat. It was a moment I will never forget.

As the last note of the song rang out, the audience jumped to their feet, many with tears on their cheeks. They clapped and cheered, the house lights flashed on and off, the stomping and cheering grew louder. The band looked at Josh, put their instruments down, stood up with huge smiles and started clapping. I did the same.

In so many ways, it was a classic Opry moment: a taste of bliss, a sustained standing ovation, a burst of joy and unity. It was also a deep acknowledgment of a single veteran's service, a thank-you to all veterans who've served, and a ninetieth birthday celebration for the longest-running musical institution America has ever known.

When we left the stage, I wanted to sneak out to the gift shop through the back of the auditorium to buy a show poster for Josh before they sold out, but I was immediately swarmed by people who'd seen the performance, many of them Vietnam veterans who wanted to thank Josh and SongwritingWith:Soldiers and hug me. I mumbled a few words about "gift shop and poster for Josh before they sold out," and suddenly a dozen people were handing me their own newly purchased show posters. I accepted one, thanked the person who gave it to me, posed for some pictures with folks, and made my way backstage to celebrate with Josh and Rob and the band. As I handed him the show poster, Josh kept shaking his head and saying how much he felt like his story could help other veterans, how he knew he was part of something bigger than himself now. He was beaming.

Muhammad Ali said, "Service to others is the rent you pay for your room here on earth." We are all renters here, mortals in temporary housing. On this night, Josh and I paid a little rent, had a little taste of heaven on earth, and connected to a sense of purpose bigger than both of us. I think of this moment whenever I feel like almost all the news on TV is bad, when we are on the verge of new wars, new terror attacks, new forms of hatred, and threats of violence and abuse from multiple kinds of brutal bullies. I'm in awe of the power of song to open us up and the power of vulnerability and emotional truth to bring us together. I am forever grateful to be a songwriter, called to song when I needed healing without knowing that the songs were coming through me to heal others, too. Songs have given me, and so many others, a new life.

After we played the Opry, Josh started making plans to ride his wheelchair for 422 miles to draw attention to veteran suicide. He chose 422 miles because he was going to do the ride "for the 22." According to the VA, America is losing 22 veterans a day to suicide, and every veteran I've worked with over the last seven years lives in fear of a 3:00 a.m. phone call telling them one of their own has taken their life. Josh hoped to raise awareness, raise money for SW:S, and let veterans know it is ok to ask for help.

During his month-long 422-mile ride from American Legion Post #31 in Angola, Indiana, to the Sportsmen's Tavern in Buffalo, New York, Josh sat for over forty media interviews and six television appearances and met people in every town he rolled through. I was there when he arrived in Buffalo with his friend and fellow veteran Roger Straide behind him in the spare wheelchair and Rob Spohr beside them on a skateboard, with a police escort in front of them, lights flashing.

Tears filled my eyes as Josh rolled in. He took my heart in his hands and opened it wider. I cried like a baby. Josh and I looked into one another's eyes and shared a deep knowing that this is what we are here for, what we humans are made to do.

After two TV interviews and photos with the local paper, Josh and I took to the stage at the Sportsmen's Tavern and we ended with our song "Still on the Ride." For the encore, we chose Woody Guthrie's "This Land Is Your Land" as the final song of the night. Josh took the harmonica solo in the middle and played it with feeling. The crowd went wild.

After the show, as we were packing to leave, the bar phone rang. The owner, a veteran of the Vietnam War, walked the phone over to Josh with a huge smile on his face and handed it to him. A man Josh had never met, the owner of a local green dry cleaner, had just seen him on TV and decided to match the money Josh had raised over the last month. It came to well over twenty thousand dollars.

A Hollywood ending to a day that gave me so many reasons to keep on believing: People are good, life has meaning, and service is its own reward.

A year later, at a show at The Linda in Albany, Josh made me cry again when I invited him to join me on stage, and he stood up, with the help of a cane, and slowly walked to the stage. I had no idea that he'd been working with a physical therapist to straighten his spine, doing hours of exercises daily to get to this point. He went on to give his badass all-terrain wheelchair to a Korean War vet who could get plenty of use out of it, and Josh is now able to walk without a cane.

People ask me if I believe songs can change the world.

My answer is yes, absolutely! How? It starts with the heart. A song can change a heart by generating empathy. To feel the feelings of another as we understand and feel our own is to become more merciful. Great songs are inseparable from empathy. A changed heart will change a mind. When a mind changes, a person changes. When a people change, the world changes. One song, one heart, one mind, one person at a time.

Song is the most distilled of all the arts, the most clarified, accessible, and democratic; anybody can connect with a song. You don't have to have gone to college. Songs transcend all manner of boundaries and speak a universal language, their message delivered in the simplest, most penetrating way. Songs speak to us in our mother tongues. They speak the language of the human heart. They can be, and are, the stepping stones we walk across through dark swamps of isolation into a simple, vital truth: we are kindred with other souls.

We are not alone.

♥

Several years ago, an elderly gentleman stood waiting at the end of the autograph line after a London show. Bent forward from time and struggle, he walked with the aid of a silver-handled walking stick. With a long white beard trimmed to a point just above his chest, black-framed trapezoid eyeglasses, a gray gangster-style fedora, a white gauze summer shirt (no collar), and a buttoned-up vest with a pocket watch chain, he resembled Sigmund Freud.

I met the intensity of his eyes, waited for him to speak.

He stood for a long moment, looking at me, tears glistening. Then he softly said, "I'm here to thank you, Mary. I live in Switzerland. Today, I came back to London for the first time in seventy years. Today, I went to the place where I was sexually abused when I was four. You have no idea the impact of your music, the courage it gives people. I want to thank you, express my gratitude."

Can you love someone in a moment? I think so, yes. My heart swung open as I took in the beauty of this brave man standing in front of me. I loved him. I reached for his hand, held it. I told him I hoped he could find peace from his childhood abuse. He nodded yes, he thinks he can, now. He leaned across the table and kissed my cheeks, one, then the other, smiled a half smile, then slowly walked away.

Epilogue

I'm a troubadour. Troubadouring is an approach, not a genre. Inside the word "troubadour," I hear the word "true." Troubadours tell true stories, true to feeling, not fact. People need stories to make meaning out of their lives, and songs are how most people get their stories. Modern-day troubadours are self-perceived outsiders who write songs about underdogs, unnoticed or marginalized folks, and struggles not often heard in mainstream music. In an age of misinformation and lies, we are the wandering minstrels who compose and perform songs to tell truths. And like the stories of old, songs help teach us how to live, and why.

Troubadours play in theaters, listening rooms, night-clubs, bars, people's homes, yards, barns, at folk festivals, on live streams, earning what we can by performing where we can. Troubadours aren't the kind of songwriters who try to write songs for hit-driven music marketplaces. We're the other kind.

When people ask me what kind of songs I write, I tell 'em I write real ones. I am called to write songs that help people check in, not out. While my songs will likely not be hits, they feed me in ways fame and money cannot. My work is more a ministry than a show business venture, though there is, of course, a show business component in every successful ministry. I've offered my opinions and observations on songwriting here with no small amount of terror. I'm no more qualified to write about songwriting than any other songwriter who has made it their life's work. I cannot read music or notate it properly. I'm not always sure of what key I'm in or what chord I'm playing. I have no idea what key I sing in, and I honestly don't care. I've carved a career from focused effort, trusting my gut, and sitting studiously at the feet of the masters. I am a teacher, but also a student. There is always more to learn about music and song.

I've played in dozens of countries and listened to thousands of people's stories, heard late-night confessions and held strangers in my arms as they wept. No matter a person's nationality, age, race, gender, sexuality, politics, religion, or lack of religion, human emotion is the same everywhere I go.

People are lonely, yearning for meaningful connection.

People need hope.

They need to believe in something.

People are hurting.

Many are traumatized, afraid.

People need love.

But love is hard, so much harder than they expected. I understand because I feel these things too.

It's why I became a troubadour.

Acknowledgments

A HUGE thank-you to Beth Langan, Allison Moorer, Carol Caldwell, early readers who encouraged me and walked me across the hot coals of unknowing. Thank you to Suzanne Kingsbury and Liz Murray, whose steadfast encouragement and faith in me helped bring this book to life. Thank you to Darrell Scott, who showed me how to teach songwriting, then encouraged me to do so. Thank you to Lydia Hutchinson, whose unwavering faith in me makes me a better teacher. I would also like to thank the maestro Michele Gazich, whose violin and viola playing have been a huge part of my music and my healing for decades, and whose love of books and bookstores knows no bounds. His encouragement helped me to stay the path with this manuscript. I would also like to thank Steve Wasserman, who came to me out of nowhere and pushed me into the dream I'd kept secret, the dream of becoming an author. His early invitation to write was the moment this book began for me, and I am forever grateful. Thank you to Elisabeth Dyssegaard for bringing that dream into full manifestation after years of wandering, and helping me sort out the vision in order to bring these pages to life.